Stabbed with a Wedge of Cheese

Stabbed with a Wedge of Cheese
of Cheese
...and Other Cultural Oddities

Charles Downey

QUILL
WILLIAM MORROW
NEW YORK

For Grace and John

It is the policy of William Morrow and Company, Inc., and its imprints and affiliates, recognizing the importance of preserving what has been written, to print the books we publish on acid-free paper, and we exert our best efforts to that end.

Library of Congress Cataloging-in-Publication Data

Downey, Charles.
    Stabbed with a wedge of cheese : . . . and other cultural oddities /
Charles Downey.
        p.   cm.
    ISBN 0-688-10899-7
    1. Curiosities and wonders.   I. Title.
AG243.D68   1992
031.02—dc20   92-8050
                                                                      CIP

Printed in the United States of America

First Quill edition

1   2   3   4   5   6   7   8   9   10

BOOK DESIGN BY LISA STOKES

CONTENTS

INTRODUCTION

Our culture is a lot richer—and zanier—than most people realize.

Americans have been accused of being many things, but from where I sit, one thing we are not is dull. Americans have tremendous fun with special holidays, daffy sports, unusual museums, dizzy vacation treats, amusing annual events, and all types of clubs. For instance, almost everybody has heard of the Kiwanis or Lions Clubs. But how many people know about the Bonehead Club or the International Save the Pun Foundation?

Stabbed with a Wedge of Cheese has no characters or plot and won't improve your love life, reduce your waistline, or increase your hairline. But it is full of unusual—and true—tidbits about cultural oddities.

The book actually started with a doornail.

Or, more accurately, a question about a doornail.

Several years ago, I bought a fixer-upper house and made the repairs on weekends. I had a constant need for nails and found there are many: ring nails, shank nails, green sinkers, roofing nails, cement nails, finishing nails, and so on. Once, I asked the hardware store owner what a doornail (from the expression "dead as a doornail") was. But he also had never heard of that type of nail. So I looked up the expression "dead as a doornail" and found, in fourteenth-century England, a doornail was the plate upon which a door knocker was struck. The doornail was said to be dead because it had been struck so hard and so often there could be no life left in it. The expression was used in the fourteenth century just as it is today. (See Chapter 8 for more ancient phrases and words we use daily. It tells how the language we speak is a slice of living history.)

For magazine articles, I often research many serious topics like reducing crime, safeguarding the planet's health, and taking better care of babies damaged before birth by illicit drugs. So for a break, I'll glance through the seventeen-pound volume *Encyclopedia of Associations* and see if the International Organization of Nerds or the National Society for the Prevention of Cruelty to Mushrooms have scheduled their annual conventions yet.

Much of a journalist's job is finding and developing ideas for feature articles. Newspapers are a great source of small items that can be greatly expanded. So, as a part of the job, I scan six newspapers daily and spot the occasional gem—many of which I've passed on to you here. I long ago quit regarding newspapers as a source of news but as a fertile ground for mini-treasure hunts.

In a world plagued with all manner of problems, my attention always seems to fall on the far-out. Thus, while a foreign war or the National Organization for Women captures the front pages of newspapers everywhere, my eye is drawn by a tiny item on the last page about the I Hate Mayonnaise Club, a group of people who think mayonnaise is a by-product of Teflon.

So although I've probably missed all the serious issues of our times and culture, I have been able to turn up quite a few treats, surprises, and oddities.

1
COCKEYED CLUBS

Groucho Marx once sent to his exclusive Hollywood club a telegram that read: "Please accept my resignation. I don't want to belong to any club that will have me as a member."

Victor Mature is said to have once applied for membership at an exclusive country club. But the management said they didn't take actors.

"I'm no actor," Mature said, "and I've got sixty-four pictures to prove it."

What Victor Mature and Groucho needed were clubs for bad actors and for comics who didn't fit in anywhere at all. It seems there are clubs for just about every other reason. If you're tall or short, handsome or homely, a lover of aardvarks, a flying funeral director, dull or adventurous, there's probably a group somewhere to share your outlook, characteristics, or hobbies.

Take adventure, for instance. If you like your sports spiced with more risk than usual, the Oxford Dangerous Sports Club of Britain may be for you. One year at a resort in Switzerland, members of the club skied down slopes in bathtubs, on stepladders, bicycles, and a grand piano, all of which were attached to skis. (Mozart was played on the way down.) Oxford club members have harnessed themselves to huge elastic ropes and then plunged off tall bridges like San Francisco's Golden Gate, where,

well, they just hung around until the thrill wore off. Despite the
flirtation with death, none of Oxford's members has been killed
or injured. During one outing, club members in formal attire
climbed to the lip of an active volcano and enjoyed a luncheon
of salad, wine, and brandy while the volcano belched sulfurous
fumes.

Aligned in spirit, if not in deed, are the two thousand members of the American Coaster Enthusiasts' Club, who tour amusement parks in search of the biggest, fastest, and scariest rides.
Moreover, once is never enough; some members will ride a truly
excellent ride or roller coaster thirty or forty times.

Completely opposed to anything at all that gets more than
four feet above the ground is the thousand-member Man Will
Never Fly Memorial Society Internationale.

"We are devoted to the proposition that birds fly and humankind drinks," says the president. The society presents an
annual award to those who do the most to discourage the idea
that flight is logical. And each year an "unknown celebrity"
speaks on the notion that the Wright Brothers never got off the
ground.

Much more lofty in aspirations is the Worldwide Association
of Space Explorers. So far, there are only two hundred members
from thirteen countries. The single requirement for joining: You
must have orbited Earth in a spacecraft at least once. It is reported
that nobody in that organization will speak to any of the four
thousand worldwide members of the Ancient Astronaut Society,
who believe Earth was visited in prehistoric times by extrater-
restrial beings.

One man's attempt at noteworthy flight led to recognition
by the seventy-two-year-old Bonehead Club of Dallas, Texas.
The Bonehead of the Year award is presented in most years to
the person—or thing—who most clearly lives up to the ideals
of the club. One year, the award was presented to a Hollywood,
California, man who attached an aluminum lawn chair to forty-
three helium balloons and sailed to sixteen thousand feet. To

land, the lawn-chair pilot carried a BB gun to shoot the balloons. He was later cited by the Federal Aviation Administration for flying at the wrong altitude. Other Bonehead awards have gone to a professional football player who ran eighty yards the wrong way for a touchdown; a thirteen-year-old girl for becoming the first girl Boy Scout; and Nelson and Bunker Hunt for cornering the silver market and losing a billion dollars. Richard Nixon was named Bonehead of the Year in 1972 for calling in a play to the Miami sideline during the Dolphins' Super Bowl loss to the Dallas Cowboys. And, more recently, the award went to the U.S. Treasury for issuing the Susan B. Anthony dollar, a coin people rarely see or use.

Another group that issues annual awards is the International Save the Pun Foundation. With honorees known as the "Ten Best Stressed Puns of the Year," the foundation recently recognized the following groaners:

"In Boston, two chefs were competing for the title Finest Fish Fryer. Their talents were about equal and their dishes excellent, so it was a close race until, at the last minute, one of the chefs glazed his entry and won the title.

"Alas!" said the other with a sigh. "There but for the glaze of cod go I."

"Speaking of fish, did you know that ancient fishing villages bartered with fish instead of money? They were the first to use credit cods."

And, finally, "Most people know the legend of William Tell, but few realize that he and his family were champion bowlers whose team was sponsored by local merchants. Even now, to be able to claim the Tells once represented your family business would have great advertising value. Unfortunately, the old records have been lost and today we can't be sure for whom the Tells bowl."

The Burlington Liars' Club of Burlington, Wisconsin, was founded in 1929 when two reporters from competing newspapers in Racine ran into a dry spell, so they collaborated on an article

12

ıg around a police station, seeing who could
liticians weren't allowed entry, according to
ᴖ, because they are considered "professional liars."
ᴖne entry from a Missouri man told about how cold it had been
that winter. "I saw a politician standing on a corner with his
hands in his own pockets." The most recent winning entry, culled
from two hundred submissions in twenty states and eight foreign
nations, was from a retired man who described how he once
received a record as a gift. The man liked the music on one side
best, and played it so many times the record became thin enough
so that music from both sides could be played at once. At one
Liars' Club meeting, a member announced that he worked for
the International Olympics as a javelin catcher. And another
member argued with a straight face that his town was so small
they had to extend the town limits to make room for a phone
booth.

The Memorandum Club collected not tall tales but examples
of wordy, unclear communications used in business and government and then made awards. The winner one year was from
Australia and read: "Officers will be obliged to adopt reconcep-
tualization in respect to any high-stream in-basket situation, and
to maintain perspective based upon an interaction matrix. Officers should parameterize upward compatible cybercrud wetware,
and sub-optimize any long-bomb hardwired binary-chop boot-
strap programs."

If you like bumbling, rather than verbose memos, the International Association of Professional Bureaucrats is for you.
Their slogan: "When in charge, ponder; when in trouble, delegate; when in doubt, mumble." The association once challenged
the U.S. Post Office by sending two letters from Philadephia to
Washington, D.C., one by regular mail and the other by a pony
express rider. The horse-carried letter won, hands down.

Also celebrating mediocrity in the American culture is the
Society for the Preservation and Enhancement of the Recognition

of Millard Fillmore, Last of the Whigs, or SPERMFLOW. Fillmore, the thirteenth U.S. president, took over the presidency on the death of Zachary Taylor in 1850 and the entire cabinet resigned in protest. Fillmore served until 1853 and had a reputation for doing nothing. Yearly, the society awards a Medal of Mediocrity, most recently given to the historian who suggested Zachary Taylor be disinterred and his body tested for poison.

Many people would feel that the National Organization Taunting Safety and Fairness Everywhere, or NOT SAFE, is a far more rational and efficient group. NOT SAFE believes if something is worth doing, it's worth overdoing. "Ninety-nine percent of all aircraft accidents could be eliminated if aircraft were required to taxi to their destinations," says Dale Lowdermilk, founder and executive director. "We think warning labels should be placed on banana peels and would like to see a speed limit of 15 mph everywhere."

Some things can take even longer than a taxiing plane heading cross-country. If you tend to let things slide, you'll want to know about the Procrastinators' Club of America. Its four thousand members celebrate Christmas in July and protested the War of 1812 in 1967. Members have found that many things need not be done at all if you just put them off long enough. Membership is open to anybody who doesn't fill out and return their application too quickly. And, when they get around to it, the Procrastinators will send you their official publication, *Last Month's Newsletter*.

"Actually, procrastinators are healthier," says club founder Less Waas. "We are less inclined to rush through life and die young. See, when you die, you're referred to as the 'late' so-and-so. We would much rather be late while we're still alive."

If it's a lack of brainpower and not procrastination that interests you, the DENSA (Diversely Educated, Not Seriously Affected) Society wants you to know they will take anybody with less than a 134 IQ, or anyone who has been rejected by

MENSA, the club for people with genius-level IQs. Instead, DENSA offers a DQ (density quotient) exam in which prospective members must fill a bathtub to its brim. "If you displace any water at all when you get into the tub, you are dense enough for us," says J. D. Stewart, chairman.

Sample questions from the official DENSA quiz book: "True or false: people who eat food live longer than people who do not eat food." "Decide which word doesn't rhyme: bar, car, far, jar, miscellaneous, star, tar." "Who doesn't fit in? George Washington, Abraham Lincoln, John Adams, Liberace." "Question: What is the speed of dark?" "How many stars are in the sky?" (Answer: all of the above). The club keeps a library containing a thesaurus, a dictionary, and a *Time* magazine. Its periodic publication is *The Snooze News*. Also, the club bestows the Golden Toad Award for public acts of denseness.

But if you don't want to spend the time studying for DENSA's entrance exams, there is the International Dull Folks Unlimited. That club is a good choice if you bought cable TV for the twenty-four-hour weather channel, if your idea of hors d'oeuvres is pretzels, and if your reversible jackets are brown on both sides. Accessories needed for the dull pride lifestyle are blackwall tires, white bread, and a collection of souvenir ashtrays. The club advances the notion that even celebrities and influential people can be uninteresting, and it opposes trendiness everywhere. "Naturally, we favor marriage over relationships," says J. D. Stewart, who is chairman of the Dull Folks as well as of DENSA.

The club maintains a Dull Hall of Fame and issues brown papers on matters of economic and social importance. The club plans to sponsor the following books: *The Browning of America*, *Dull Men Eat Anything*, and a dullest-rated *Almanac*, which lists the least lively cities in the United States.

"You know you're dull if you drink generic beer, your favorite piece of furniture is a La-Z-Boy recliner, and if you truly believe there's always room for Jell-O," Stewart says.

In opposition to Stewart's group is the Boring Institute, whose many members struggle against boredom in all its forms. The Institute publishes a pamphlet, *Ten Secrets to Avoid Boredom*, a paperback book, *Boring Stuff—How to Spot It, How to Avoid It*, and a Boring Certificate suitable for framing. The institute honors the year's most yawn-inspiring celebrities and films.

Closely allied with the Boring Institute is the National Anxiety Center, which every year presents its Chicken Little Award to the person or fad that has done the most to promote anxiety in America. The award most recently went to a scientist who wrongly predicted a massive earthquake near Memphis, Tennessee, demonstrating "that anyone with a Ph.D. can be given free rein to create a high level of public anxiety."

Promoting more anxiety than almost anybody is the Committee for Immediate Nuclear War, a group that promotes global nuclear war as a solution to problems like boredom, soap operas, and peddlers on New York City's Fourteenth Street.

If you feel you're having too much fun, there is The Society for Secular Armageddonism, a group dedicated to letting everybody know "the end of the world is at hand." A DOOM hotline—with screams and groans in the background—promises to ruin your day by reciting all the reasons why the world's end is close at hand.

Trying to eliminate doom and gloom is Joygerms Unlimited of Syracuse, New York. The club wants to rid the world of gruff and grumpy grouches by promoting goodwill. It holds an annual Joygerm Parade, while the Hug Club provides necessary support. Also working on the elimination of gloom was the American Zombie Association, whose 102 members are concerned with preserving the alcoholic drink, "The Zombie."

Preserving an era, and not exotic drinks, is the idea of the 70s Preservation Society. If you liked disco, flared jeans, the TV show *Welcome Back, Kotter*, and lava lamps, the club may be right for you.

Ladies Against Women (LAW) wants to preserve the good

old days of male superiority, conducts workshops for "uppity women," and holds consciousness-lowering sessions. LAW organizes bake sales for the Pentagon, advocates banning books instead of bombs, and wants to see a national dress code adopted.

Another disgruntled group is seeking respectability, even though their letterhead is printed upside down and they insist on enlisting members against their will. The International Society of Nerds boasts about seven thousand members, all of whom consider nerdity a mark of distinction. Most became members when well-meaning friends sent their names to club headquarters in Cincinnati, Ohio. Bruce Chapman, Supreme Archnerd of the club, says he often goes by the name A. B. Nerdling while wearing a fright wig, a pair of large glasses held together with tape, a plastic pocket pen holder containing thirty-seven ballpoints, and shirts and slacks of clashing plaids. A kindred group, The Society of Nerds and Geeks at Harvard University, was formed to fight the forces of anti-intellectualism.

If the thing you're fighting is termination, you may be interested in The Loyal Order of Swine Singers, an association of executives and other workers whose careers have been disrupted by corporate takeovers.

"Kindly observe that the acronym for our club is LOSS," says David Workman, of Winston-Salem, North Carolina, a region that has been hit hard by corporate takeovers and mergers. Workman lost his airline job after the airline was taken over by a larger carrier. "We hit on Swine Singers because of the old saying, 'Never teach a pig to sing. All you do is waste your time and annoy the pig.' " The club's Latin motto is Totus porkus, or Whole hog. Although the club is a loose-knit support group and social network, the Swine Singers are developing special traditions such as a club signal whereby one finger is placed under the nose while uttering a discreet grunt.

The National Chastity Association is a social club and dating service for those who eschew premarital sex, kissing, and even hand-holding. According to the club's "Nineteen Desires," you cannot truly be in love until after marriage.

Man Watchers, with headquarters in Hollywood, California, has ten thousand female members who appreciate and openly ogle a well-turned male form. Members present "Well Worth Watching" cards to men they find especially attractive, and produce America's Most Watchable Men competitions.

In the interest of controlling rather than celebrating human impulses, Messies Anonymous is dedicated to helping the overwhelmed get, and stay, organized. Most of the six thousand members use the group's bible, *The Messies Manual*, to learn about such revolutionary techniques as the Mount Vernon Method of Cleaning, which is said to have been used at the home of George Washington to keep order.

Compulsive savers have a Pack Rats Anonymous support group in southern California for people who hoard stacks of newspapers and other junk items. A weekly meeting starts like an Alcoholics Anonymous program with the problem saver standing before the group, announcing: "Hi, I'm Joe and I'm a pack rat." Research has shown that 10 percent of the population suffers from compulsive saving.

The National Frumps of America Club has ten thousand members including Barbara Bush and Roseanne Barr. "Frumpdom is basically a desire for comfortable footwear," says Frump founder and president Barbara Hovanetz, who claims your "Frump Quotient" can be found in "yes" answers to the following quiz: Do you enjoy reading garden catalogs; have dinner at the coffee table while watching Jeopardy; and trim coupons from the newspaper exactly along the dotted lines? Do you find roadside tourist attractions irresistible; own several pieces of Elvis memorabilia; use a measuring cup as a soup ladle; wear oversized T-shirts and baggy pants instead of dieting; and is most of your wardrobe made up from K-Mart Blue Light specials? Hovanetz says the organization was founded in 1964 when six undergraduate friends who had never dated became interested in bric-a-brac, life insurance, and the miles per gallon their cars were getting. Since then, helpful hints and features have been printed in the club newsletter, the *Frump Update*.

"I always say you should be proud because Frump stands for 'Frugal, Reliable, Unpretentious, Mature Persons,' " Hovanetz says.

Opposed to any technology or program offered in behalf of television is the Society for the Eradication of Television (SET). The club's 350 members refuse to own a TV and hope all others will be dumped into an ocean. SET claims that television "retards inner life, destroys human interaction, squanders time, and draws viewers into abject addiction."

The Visual Lunacy Society is not concerned with television screens but with rubber stamps as mail art and as an act of rebellion against a bureaucratic society. The society creates and distributes rubber stamps such as "Returned, Signature of the Pope Required," and "Resubmit, in Arabic."

Other clubs are dedicated to the special needs of people who are tall, short, fearful, sarcastic, and bald.

With a battle cry of "No drugs, plugs or rugs!" ten thousand members of the Bald Headed Men of America want to convince you that skin is in. The club stresses that members should believe that "Bald is Beautiful" and there is no need to pull out their few remaining strands over the lack of a perfect cure for baldness.

"We feel America has had enough of cover-ups," says John T. Capps III, club president.

New York City's Bald Urban Liberation Brigade (BULB), inspired by gay "outing" campaigns, names celebrities and politicians who have tried to keep their baldness a secret. BULB altered and published their pictures to show what the men look like without hairpieces.

The International Tall Club has forty-five local branches in the United States and Canada, including the Towering Texans, headquartered in Dallas. Life is filled with minor annoyances for women members, who stand over five foot ten, and for men, who must be at least six foot two to join. Tall Club members often raise their kitchen and bathroom sinks to avoid back pain and must put up with car seats that won't slide back far enough.

For small people, life's awkward moments are reversed, so Richard Crandall, a three-foot-ten businessman, founded the Short Stature Foundation to unite little people with the rest of society. There is also the five thousand-member Little People of America.

The National Association to Advance Fat Acceptance offers tips for the overweight on dealing with discrimination and hints on where to find large sizes in business outfits and other apparel.

If your concern is an overly sharp tongue or unconsciously sneering remarks, Sarcastics Anonymous can teach you the positive uses of sarcasm. Club founder Virginia Tooper, who considers herself a "recovering sarcastic," says the club is for people who are stuck living or working with sarcastic "significant others." Tooper, a former college professor who lectures on humor and sarcasm, says she is married to a master sarcastic who once spray painted some of her freshly cooked meatballs and hung them on a Christmas tree. Tooper is presently collecting all she's learned in a book, *How to Practice Safe Sarcasm and Stop Humor Abuse*.

If your other skills—like advanced eye crossing or yodeling—are lacking, you may want to know about The Institute of Totally Useless Skills in Dover, New Hampshire. Rick Davis, who claims to be a professor of Totally Useless Skills, says he has written a text that contains instructions on spoon playing, unusual finger-snapping routines, and all sorts of "boggles," an example of which is rubbing your stomach and patting your head at the same time. Another boggle Davis teaches: drawing a circle in the air with one finger while the other sketches a box.

Gone, but not forgotten by their members, are defunct clubs like Parents of Hippies; the Witchdoctors' Club; the Backscratchers of America; the Convicts' Association for a Good Environment; the Commission for Zero Automobile Growth; the National Indigestion Society; Sports Fans Totally Against Blimps; the Society for the Preservation of Poultry Antiquities; United Ancient Order of Druids; the Worldwide Cuspidor Hitters' Association; The Society of Dirty Old Men.

Says Bob Armstrong, founder and ex-director of the now-defunct Couch Potatoes: "I hated to disband the club but running the organization was cutting into my TV-watching time too much."

If you own a plane and use it in your work, your choice of associations is wide. There are: Flying Funeral Directors of America; Flying Dentists; Flying Pharmacists; Flying Parsons; the International Society of Flying Engineers; Flying Teen Farmers; the International Flying Nurses' Association; and the Flying Chiropractors' Association.

It used to be that a person with an unusual collection was known as an eccentric. Today, when any two such collectors meet, it seems they create a club. For instance, the Lilliputian Bottle Club is for people who collect miniature liquor bottles like those served on planes. One member claims to have twenty thousand bottles, some of which are shaped like King Tut and Laurel and Hardy. The Count Dracula Society collects literature about horror films and maintains a Horror Hall of Fame. The Amphibious Auto Club of America collects cars that travel on both water and asphalt, while the GWTW (Gone With The Wind) Collectors' Club seeks and keeps memorabilia used in making the epic 1939 movie.

The Cannon Hunters' Association of Seattle looks for ancient, large-bore muzzleloaders so they can restore and display them. Much more romantic is the National Valentine Collectors' Association, which was organized to help members buy, sell, and trade tokens of affection from bygone days. The Golden Glow of Christmas Past is a national organization for collectors of Christmas memorabilia. The International Barbed Wire Collectors' Association saves eighteen-inch hunks of barbed wire from fifteen countries. Other clubs collect Ronald Reagan Borax ads or Dr. Pepper bottles. The 250-member Texas Date Nail Collectors' Association collects the massive nails that are driven into railroad ties.

The Beer Can Collectors of America collects both opened and unopened beer cans. The cans are traded among members but never sold.

Other collector organizations gather Chinese snuff bottles, Japanese swords, frisbees, bricks, hatpins, corkscrews, keys, lighters, decoys, toothpick holders, inkwells, sparkplugs, thermometers, thimbles, and matchbooks. The Occupied Japan Club collects anything stamped "Made in Occupied Japan."

The Society for Advancing the Art of Civility and the Art of Cultural Harmony collected examples of public rudeness. The society was founded by a California realtor reacting to boorish, unmannerly drivers of cars and supermarket shopping carts.

Perhaps because rudeness has been around as long as human beings have (and promises never to become outdated), it is not a feature of the Society for Creative Anachronism. This nostalgic organization promotes swordplay, jousting, and other medieval cultural and sporting delights.

Writer Larry Orrenstein once looked in history books and created the Club of Odd Ends, a group for whom death came somewhat strangely. Among other Odd Enders, Orrenstein found the case of a thirty-six-year-old woman who decided to murder her twenty-three-year-old husband, a Marine Corps drill instructor, to collect his twenty-thousand-dollar life insurance policy. She baked him a pie containing the venom sac of a tarantula, then tried to electrocute him in the shower, poison him with lye, run over him with a car, make him hallucinate while driving by putting amphetamines in his beer, and, finally, injecting an air bubble into his veins with a hypodermic needle. But nothing was done properly. Finally, she and a woman accomplice beat him over the head with a metal weight while he slept. And that did the job. In 1978, Orrenstein found the case of a Parisian grocer who stabbed his wife to death with a (presumably frozen) wedge of Parmesan cheese. In 1984, another Odd Ender joined the club when a New Zealand man killed his wife by jabbing her repeatedly in the stomach with a frozen sausage. That same year, a forty-one-year-old Pennsylvania man was asphyxiated after his 280-pound wife sat on his chest after an argument. Eight months later, a forty-one-year-old Indiana woman beat her male companion to death by repeatedly dropping a bowling ball on his head while he lay on the floor in front of a television set. In Czechoslovakia, a woman who might have wanted to join the Club of Odd Ends jumped from a third-story window after learning her husband had been unfaithful. But she landed on the husband, who was entering the building at that moment. "He died instantly. She survived," writes Orrenstein.

Other Odd Enders include a man in Los Angeles who put a gun to his head and pulled the trigger. However, the bullet passed through his head, ricocheted off a water heater, and struck his female companion between the eyes.

But if nothing at all sounds like fun, there's always the National Association for the Humor Impaired. Dr. Humor, who in real life is Stu Robertshaw, a University of Wisconsin-La Crosse psychology professor, says life is less rich if you can't laugh. To test your laugh quotient, Robertshaw offers what he calls "Dr. Humor's Quick-Score Test for Humor Impairment." The twenty-item test consists of statements like, "Never try to pick up a woman who is wearing a Super Bowl ring . . . " "It is in bad taste to inquire whether you are in the will of a suicidal person . . . " and "I'd give my right arm to be ambidextrous." Failure to smile at such statements, according to Robertshaw, may indicate a humor impairment. Thus, membership includes a certificate, wallet card, and information about "treatment" for humor impairment. Dr. Humor also ministers to some groups—notably, lawyers and school administrators—in whom levity often isn't a highly developed attribute.

Liverwurst eaters of the world, unite!

Some clubs are dedicated to food. For instance, the Society for the Restoration and Preservation of Red M&Ms was formed when the Mars company stopped making them. The National Society for Prevention of Cruelty to Mushrooms was formed to prevent unkind acts to mushrooms. The International Banana Club wants people everywhere to smile more in a world that is "going bananas." To help, the club maintains a library and museum of over twelve thousand banana artifacts, and awards a Master and Doctorate of Bananistry.

For those who like their foods with a little more spice, there are the Chili Appreciation Society International, and Chili-U.S.A. Local chapters, or "pods," host chili cook-offs and elect a Great Pepper, or president, to guide chili doings.

The three-thousand-member World Pumpkin Confederation concentrates on growing massive vegetables. To date, members of the confederation have turned in a pumpkin weighing 833 pounds, a watermelon that tipped the scales at 262 pounds, a 124-pound cabbage, and one radish that weighed in at 28.1 pounds. The confederation's goal is to grow a 1,000-pound pumpkin by the year 2000.

Lovers of garlic can join a special interest group, Lovers of the Stinking Rose. Potato Eaters just get together and eat all types of spuds.

No Mayo News, the newsletter of the I Hate Mayonnaise Club, is for people who want to have a list of mayo-free restaurants.

"Right now it's pretty bleak because Pizza Hut is the only one," says club president Charles Memminger of Honolulu.

Readers of *No Mayo News*, in all states and two nations, share everything from traumatic experiences with mayo to helpful disposal hints. One reader from Allentown, Pennsylvania, wrote in to say he uses mayo to remove old bumper stickers. Yet another reader waxed philosophic and mused, "Cats and dogs won't eat mayo, why should humans?"

Memminger, who has always claimed that mayonnaise is a by-product of Teflon, says contributors receive a "Just Say No Mayo" bumper sticker.

But if you object to the entire fast-food culture, you may want to know about the twenty-thousand-member Slow Food International. That organization wants to spread the word about the joys of leisurely dining. Founded in 1986 to protest a McDonald's opening in Rome, the New York City-based group now opposes most plastic because it allows rapid dining in fast food joints.

For years, getting membership in the now-defunct Custard Pie Society simply required going to a restaurant with at least two other people and consuming a whole custard pie directly from the pie plate after eating a full dinner.

What's in a name?

Increasingly, people who are sensitive about their names are banding together in clubs and societies. One group wants their names to be no longer associated with bathroom fixtures. The Association to Deter People from Calling Toilets John (A.T.D.P.F.C.T.J.) is open to people who have John as a first, middle, or last name.

"By the way, the 'Johns' who go to prostitutes are a completely different club," says club chairman John Jackson of Chatsworth, California. The group wears hats with the association's initials and gives out cards asking people not to call toilets "johns."

The George Club, based in San Antonio, Texas, claims among its members President George Bush, comic George Burns, author George Plimpton, commentator George Will, and the mayor of Georgeville, Texas. The club meets annually on George Washington's birthday to select the George of the Year. Most recently, George Bush defeated boxer George Foreman (who named each of his five sons George). Previously, George

Wendt, who plays Norm on TV's *Cheers*, was named George of the Year.

A more exclusive organization is the Jim Smith Society. The club offers data on Jim Smiths throughout history and sponsors an occasional "Jim Smith of the Year Award."

But perhaps the most exclusive (and self-effacing) of all is the Denis Thatcher Society, an organization of little-known husbands of famous women that was formed by Jim Schroeder, husband of Representative Pat Schroeder of Colorado. (Denis Thatcher, patron saint of the obscure, is the retiring spouse of Margaret Thatcher, Britain's former prime minister.) The Washington, D.C., club—whose motto is "Yes, dear"—admits men whose wives are much more prominent and influential than they. Says a club spokesman: "The society is designed to help these men maintain the obscurity they have worked so hard to earn."

Partial to platypuses?

Many clubs and organizations are concerned about animals. For instance, the five hundred members of the Bat Conservation International are devoted to telling a skeptical world about the many good points of bats. Most people don't realize it, but bat society is maternal. Moreover, rabies are so rare among the flying mammals that Indian children frequently kept pet bats on a string. A common misconception is that bats suck blood or fly into your hair. According to experts, bats can learn to recognize a human's voice.

Members of the American Council of Spotted Asses are usually donkey or burro owners. However, owning a spotted ass is not as easy as acting like one. According to the club, there are only 450 spotted asses registered worldwide.

Ordinary donkeys with no spots at all have their admirers and defenders, too. The Association of Friends of Donkeys, in Germany, was formed to improve the public's image of donkeys. The club wants everybody to know that donkeys have suffered unearned prejudice. The creatures are actually neither stubborn nor asinine. For instance, when a donkey halts against his master's wishes, it only means the animal senses danger and is not being unduly obstinate. Under the same circumstances, a horse would bolt.

Another group of dedicated animal lovers is the American Association of Aardvark Aficionados. Their motto: It's aardvark, but it's worth it.

The International Order of the Armadillo wants to tell the public about the cultural and ecological value of the armadillo, a small burrowing mammal indigenous to the semitropical regions of the Americas. The armadillo only fights when attacked, and eats pests.

Other animal clubs include: Retired Greyhounds as Pets, the National Pygmy Goats Association, the National Committee on the Prairie Chicken, the Draft Horse & Mule Association of America, the Coalition for Drug-Free Horse Racing, and Tattoo-a-Pet. The Unicorn Hunters United became extinct after many years of searching for one.

The Great American Mutt Club (GAMC) of Coconut Grove, Florida, celebrates that most American creature, the mutt, and offers "Pet-a-Gree" papers to any dog owner who applies. Examples include a boxer–springer spaniel mix registered at the GAMC as a "box spring." Another pooch whose ancestry is poodle and pug is listed as a "puddle."

Says GAMC founder and president, Skip Van Cel: "My own dog is half golden retriever and half border collie. So he's registered as a 'golden deceiver.' "

Among GAMC's registry are two three-legged dogs. Both are named "Tripod."

A defunct club, the Worldwide Fair Play for Frogs Committee, wanted to protect frogs everywhere against undue harassment. But be sure not to confuse the above with the Frog Prince Conspiracy, a club for very attractive men and women.

2
ANNUAL EVENTS OF SUSPECT SIGNIFICANCE

The Russian novelist Maksim Gorky, while visiting the United States, was taken to Coney Island in New York City. The huge amusement park was thronged with tourists in a holiday mood. Gorky and his hosts spent the whole day in a whirlwind of rides, exhibits, games, and shows, taking part in almost everything the park has to offer.

As they were leaving, somebody asked Gorky what he thought about the place. The Russian writer thought for a moment and said while shaking his head in wonder: "What a sad people you must be!"

Actually, Americans go to much greater lengths to relieve their everyday woes. They hold scores of annual events that can be entertaining and more bizarre than Coney Island itself.

For instance, there's the International Strange Music Festival, conducted yearly near Olive Hill, Kentucky. "The idea of the festival is to make music from non-musical items," says organizer John Tierney, a naturalist at Carter Caves, the festival site.

One year a Japanese trio took top honors. Their winning entry, "My Old Kentucky Home," was played on a table, tea pot, and some assorted pots and pans. The table was turned upside down and strung like a cello; a reed was inserted in the tea pot so that brassy notes emanated from the spout. The pots and pans were played like bongo drums. Also featured at the festival was a fifteen-piece orchestra of automobile horns that blared out a soulful rendition of "Cherry Pink, Apple Blossom White."

In the most recent festival, a professional musician took his barn apart to make an instrument that took top honors, again, for a rendition of "My Old Kentucky Home." The device was known as a "Barn-Board Dulcimer." The real showstopper, however, was the "Humongaphonia," a bulky instrument that required three people to operate. The notes came from a slide whistle that extended to seven feet when played. Another crowd-pleaser was the "Graduated Clanger," a system of ever-smaller fire alarm bells arranged closely together and played like an xylophone. The graduated clanger rang out a traditional folk classic, "Boiling Cabbage Down."

For twelve years, the International Whistle-Off featured performers like a man who could whistle a Bach concerto as well as popular tunes like "Wave" or "Green Dolphin Street." This contestant had whistled with orchestras in Houston and Indianapolis and often won top honors at the Whistle-Off. In the most recent contest, the performance of a woman who whistled several tunes while standing on her head and conducting a puppet show with her feet brought the audience to its feet.

The National Hollerin' Contest, held yearly in June at Spivey's Corner, North Carolina, isn't exactly singing but neither is it screaming or yelling. Promoters say the idea of the contest is to revive that lost art of communication which flourished in rural America until the 1920s when the telephone came into much wider use.

The Annual Bizarre Collections Contest in Sacramento, California, has now been held for three years. At one contest a carpenter entered his collection of tidbits from the world of rock 'n' roll. That included a jellybean once stepped on by former

Beatle John Lennon and a hair snatched from the bobcat vest of Sonny Bono back when he sang with Cher.

Second place in the last contest was taken by a thirty-year-old collection of odd toothbrushes. The overall winner collected a hundred-dollar prize for his collection of coprolites—that's fossilized dinosaur dung. Among the other 124 entries were: a batch of ten thousand cigar bands; a box of fifty thousand alcoholic beverage labels gathered over fifty years; 202 unbroken wishbones saved from family dinners; a handful of skins shed by a pet tarantula named Tula; a treasure chest of lost combs; and a collection of 239 different brands of disposable cigarette lighters. One woman entered a collection of letters written to her by heartbroken men after she quit seeing them. Yet another woman had saved the metal ends of orange juice cans. Another runner-up had a collection of 448 plastic charms garnered from gumball machines.

The World Grits Festival is usually held in April at St. George, South Carolina. It's the world's only celebration honoring the South's most representative food. Not only are special grits dishes offered for breakfast, lunch, and dinner, there are: a grits mill, a grits-eating contest, and a cooking contest that showcases new recipes made of, well . . . you get the idea by now.

The most beloved event there is the Roll-in-Grits Contest. A kiddy-style wading pool is filled with hot water from a carwash and several hundred pounds of dry grits, and stirred with a canoe paddle. The object is to wallow in the pool for seven seconds and see how many pounds of grits stick to your body. Contestants are weighed before and after the event to determine the winner. While the winner one year raised some eyebrows by stuffing the mush into his pockets and picking up thirteen pounds, the winning entry of all time had twenty-six pounds of grits stuck to his body.

The festival was organized six years ago when St. George decided some type of event was needed to raise cash and boost the town's image. But most typical Southern themes—chitlins, watermelon, fried chicken, peaches, moonshine, dim-witted county sheriffs with pot bellies, and the like—were already taken. The answer, and the birth of the World Grits Festival, was found when somebody discovered that St. George's twenty-three hundred citizens were buying eighteen hundred pounds of grits a week.

Among the winning new recipes offered at the most recent gathering: grits and sausage, Swiss grits bake, and peachy grits cheesecake.

If, however, grits are not your favorite dish, your choice of other yearly fests with a food theme is considerable. There are annual festivals devoted to: apples, apple butter, applejack, asparagus, bagels, beer, blueberries, bratwurst, brussels sprouts, burro barbecue, cabbage, dates, dry beans from California, carrots, catfish, cheese, cherries, chili, chocolate, clam chowder, crabs, crayfish, dates, eels, eggs, egg salad, figs, gourmet coffee, gumbo, ham, honey, horseradish, ice cream, lobsters, maple syrup, mushrooms, oysters, peaches, peanuts, pecans, poke salad, popcorn, potatoes, pretzels, red beans and rice, rhubarb, shrimp, strawberries, sweet corn, tomatoes, watermelons, squid, snails, and rattlesnakes.

But even if you're on a diet, you can still take part in several yearly food activity affairs. There are two contests in which watermelon seeds are spit for distance. A prune-spitting championship is held at the annual Prairie Dog Chili Cook-off and World Championship of Pickled Quail Egg Eating in Grand Prairie, Texas. Top honors in this event, officially called the Cuzin Homer Page Invitational Eat-and-Run Stewed Prune Pit Spitting Contest, once went to a man who propelled a prune pit from his lips a record thirty feet, eight inches. This same festival is always finished with a Hat Stomping Contest which requires contestants to "take a perfectly good hat and destroy it in less than thirty seconds."

How would you like to drop your boss or mother-in-law into a five-hundred-gallon vat of partially congealed gelatin in front of thousands of onlookers? Of course, your boss or mother-in-law would have to go along with it and the stunt will set you back at least fifty dollars. The Houston, Texas, chapter of the Leukemia Society of America holds the Annual World's Largest Gelatin Slide to raise funds. Top-money earners of the year may name the person of their choice to be dropped into the vat. Many of the three hundred dunkees protect their dignity by wearing Halloween costumes but others wear their Sunday best for the gooey occasion.

The Twins Days Festival has been held every August in Twinsburg, Ohio, for over fifteen years. The most recent event featured nine sets of twins from the Soviet Union, as well as twin rappers Glennis and Lennis Brown, who perform under the name Twin's Hype. Twin Elvis impersonators also appeared. The fest honors the founders of Twinsburg, Aaron and Moses Wilcox, identical twins and business partners who married sisters, died of the same ailment on the same day in 1827, and are buried in the same grave. Twins attending the festival may compete in fifty-two different categories. The 1990 gathering produced an award-winning documentary, a 212-minute film, *Twinsburg, Ohio: Some Weird Kind of Twin Thing*. The film was produced by twin sisters Sue and Michelle Marcoux, students at Stanford University.

On New Year's Day in Pasadena, California, blind twins John and Larry Gassman cover the world-famous Rose Parade for public radio station KPCC. The Gassmans have a thrice-weekly radio program about old shows from radio's golden age in the thirties and forties. An estimated several hundred thousand blind and visually impaired people tune in over National Public Radio on January 1 to hear the Gassmans describe to their listeners how a particular float feels or smells when it comes by in the parade. For instance, one float featured pompano, a thick grass that reminded one brother of a horse's mane. The Gassmans know how the floats feel and smell because they've gone over

them before the parade starts. When Sea World entered a float
one year, the Gassmans were allowed to feel the inside of a killer
whale's mouth. "It feels like a row of pitchforks," says John. "Its
tongue is the size of a side of beef but feels like sandpaper."

Another overwhelming sensory experience is the annual
Rotten Sneaker Contest in Montpelier, Vermont, because it requires two exceptionally smelly and tattered tennis shoes to win.
Most entrants are energetic teens who prepare their entries by
hiking without socks in the desert, using their sneakers as brakes
for a bicycle or a motorcycle, "messing around in the lake," and
holding tug-of-war contests with large, salivating dogs, using
sneakers instead of rope. Usually, the winning tattered sneakers
hang onto the feet of the contestants by threads. Because the
winner is selected on the basis of truly repulsive odor and overall
degree of shoe raggedness, judges have been known to appraise
the entrants from a distance.

One event guaranteed not to wear out shoes is the World's
Shortest Saint Patrick's Day Parade, held every March 17 in
Maryville, Missouri. The most recent parade route measured
103 feet and was painted green. Promoters say the parade is
shortened every year so it can always set a new world's record.

For fourteen years, the Oz Festival has been held in Chit-
tenango, New York, the birthplace of author L. Frank Baum.
Although most members of the cast in the 1939 MGM classic
The Wizard of Oz have died, two of the original Munchkins were
flown in for the most recent festival. Chittenango, which lies
fifteen miles east of Syracuse, is noted for its Tinman Hardware
Store, End of the Rainbow Gift Shop, and Emeraldland City
Lanes Bowling Center (in the movie it was called the Emerald
City). One confectionery store serves Oz Cream Cones.

Gadget bashing is featured on April Fool's Eve in South
Pasadena, California. At the third annual Electro-Bash, frustrated consumers tossed Teletypes, typewriters, and all manner
of electronic devices from a second-story balcony in an event

known as the "Slam Dunk." Organizers say the event was first held to battle a nervous condition described as "consumer electronics stress syndrome." Lined up for destruction at the most recent bash were a television that conked out during the NCAA basketball playoffs, a clock radio whose alarm worked only occasionally, an answering machine that never took a message, and a cassette player that required nine different cords. One man heaved a television while it played, thanks to a very long extension cord. A video camera recorded the plunge so that the doomed TV could televise its own destruction. The second half of the event is known as the "Sledge-O-Matic," wherein sledgehammer-wielding participants, wearing protective glasses, smash their least favorite gadgets, gizmos, gimcracks, and contraptions. As one man went after his broken-down computer with a sledgehammer, the crowd cheered him on, shouting, "Hit Return key! Hit Shift! Do Escape! Alt-Delete! Run-Stop! Hit Help key!" At the most recent Electro-Bash, participants toted a bowling ball to the second-story balcony and dropped it on the lackluster electronic goods sitting below.

During Secretaries' Week in April, Manchester, New Hampshire, holds a Secretary Typewriter Toss Contest, in which frustrated secretaries heave a typewriter as far as possible.

Many annual happenings are events of the mind and the written word.

For instance, every year the American Council of Teachers of English give "doublespeak" awards to those who pretend to communicate but do not. Doublespeak is something like the concept of "doublethink" ("war is peace," "death is life") and "newspeak," expressions coined by British author George Orwell to show how language can wear a false face.

One year, a U.S. Air Force colonel won a doublespeak award for calling a Titan II missile (tipped with a nine-megaton nuclear warhead) "a very large, potentially disruptive re-entry system." Another award went to the U.S. Environmental Protection

Agency, where nobody seemed to be worried about acid rain. Instead, it was "poorly buffered precipitation" that turns lakes and rivers into vinegar.

"The Pentagon has replaced the word 'peace' with 'a state of permanent pre-hostility,'" says William Lutz, chairman of the English department at Rutgers University in New Brunswick, New Jersey. "War has been referred to as 'violence processing,' while troops are no longer surrounded or ambushed. Instead, they 'engage the enemy on all sides.' Moreover, modern soldiers are never outnumbered, they just 'operate in a target-rich environment.'"

Professor Lutz is also editor of the *Quarterly Review of Doublespeak* and has collected from all areas of life many prime examples of doublespeak, and what they really mean.

BUSINESS
Form persuader...........................girdle
Environmental hygienist ....janitor
Earth-engaging equipment ....plows
Data transport system ....briefcase

EDUCATION
Movement experience ....sports
Grapho-motor representation ....handwriting
Disparate negative import ....discrimination
Physical freeway............................hall

HEALTH
Compensated edentia....................false teeth
Activity boosters ....amphetamines
Nutritional-avoidance therapy ....diet
Negative patient care outcome ....death

GOVERNMENT
Nonecological boundary ....fence
Mobile mountain range technician..........cowboy

Natural amenity unit.....................outhouse
Adverse weather visibility device...windshield wiper
Revenue enhancement......................taxes

MILITARY
Prematurely terminated flight................crash
Overt human collection sources................spy
Philosophically disillusioned.............frightened
Ultimate high-intensity warfare........ nuclear war

Says Dr. Lutz: "Would anybody at all remember U.S. states-man Ben Franklin if he had said, '. . . in this world, nothing is certain but negative patient care outcome and revenue enhance-ment'?"

And who would have read anything by the great Russian writer Tolstoy if he had penned a book entitled "Violence Processing and a State of Permanent Pre-Hostility"?

The Society for the Preservation of English Language and Literature, or SPELL, makes a yearly Dunce Cap award for eye-catching blunders in the language. One year, the Dunce Cap went to a Japanese company for a warning label stuck on the knives they export. It read: "Caution! Blade Extremely Sharp! Keep Out of Children!" Another year, the Dunce Cap went to a publication that carried an ad announcing a theater production of "The Little Shop of Whores."

A yearly contest that wants to confuse is the Bulwer-Lytton Fiction Contest whose purpose is to compose the most putrid prose possible. The contest is named for author Edward George Bulwer-Lytton whose wordy prose included the opening to a novel, "It was a dark and stormy night," a phrase that became a staple in the cartoon feature Snoopy. The most recent winner, selected from eight thousand entries, was a woman who used sixty-nine words to describe a wheat field on a hot day. Her entry read:

"Sultry it was and humid, but no whisper of air caused the

plump laden spears of golden grain to nod their burdened heads
as they unheedingly awaited the cyclic plunder of their gleaming
treasure, while overhead the burning orb of luminescence as-
cended to its ever upward path toward a sweltering celestial apex
for, although it is not in Kansas that our story takes place, it
looks godawful like it."

Confusing terminology is not limited to America. A woman in London, England, once noticed that some potato
chips she purchased were purple. So she wrote to the company,
asking why.

The firm explained: "Potato varieties with pigmented skins
owe their color to anthocyanins dissolved in the cell sap of the
periderm and cells of the peripheral cortex."

For that letter, the Plain English Campaign bestowed one of
its six-inch "Golden Bull" awards on the firm.

Annually in May, Ditch Day descends on the normally
placid campus of California Institute of Technology in Pasadena,
California. Seniors lock freshman dormitory rooms with all types
of electronic guardians while freshmen, crazed with the prospect
of the approaching summer vacation, contrive ways to get into
the rooms. The wily seniors leave "stacks," or puzzles—long lists
of clues, humiliating chores, and technical problems to solve in
order to open the doors. (The puzzles are known as stacks because, in the days of low technology, Caltech seniors merely
stacked tons of furniture against their doors.) Thus, a visitor on
campus during the event is likely to see sights like a normally
passive nineteen-year-old physics genius using an electric saw to
cut the roof from a car. (That student then found a note from
the car's senior owner instructing the freshman to drive the car
to Santa Barbara to join a beach party.) Or a usually reserved
engineering student might dip a massive electronic combination
lock into a bucket of liquid nitrogen and then gleefully smash
the now-brittle lock to smithereens. One of the most imaginative
stacks was a three-page physics problem left taped to a door along
with a computer that had no operating instructions at all. After

working on the problem all day, the freshman discovered the door would open automatically if only it were left untouched for ten minutes.

College engineering students usually go about their work remembering the maxim KISS ("Keep It Simple, Stupid"). But during the annual Rube Goldberg Machine Contest at Purdue University, machines are designed to accomplish the simplest of tasks by going through dozens of unnecessary steps.

The Goldberg contest was reborn in 1983, when an engineering fraternity discovered that it had been popular from 1949 to 1955 while Goldberg, a cartoonist noted for drawing machines of absurd complexity to do simple tasks, was still alive. Goldberg won a Pulitzer prize for his cartoons and said his machines were "symbols of man's capacity for exerting maximum effort to accomplish minimal results."

The RGCMs (Rube Goldberg Contest Machines) at Purdue have included overly intricate devices to sharpen pencils (thirty-four steps), put a lid on a jar (forty-two steps), and gizmos that eventually put out cigarettes, open cola bottles, break eggs, and apply stamps to envelopes. As a sign of the times, solar cells, robotic arms, laser beams, electric eyes, and computers have augmented the gears, wires, ramps, pulleys, and pumps that Goldberg always relied on.

The winning entry, "The Greatest Thing Since Sliced Bread," took a $250 prize and a trophy. It produced toast by going through steps incorporating a model of the Statue of Liberty, the space shuttle, and a mousetrap, to trigger an electric train that finally dropped two slices of bread into a toaster. As the bread browned, a mechanical rabbit hopped down a bunny trail, followed by a replica of the Purdue power plant smokestack, which then fell into a bucket, causing the school's mascot, "Purdue Pete," to fly up a pole and raise an American flag. Finally, an M1 tank turned around, triggered a switch to reverse the train, and then pulled the toast from the toaster, forty-one steps later. A rap tune, "I Love Toast," played all the while.

*   *   *

Of course, many annual festivals celebrate the natural rather than the man-made. For instance, Talkeetna, Alaska, offers a Moose Dropping Festival in July. During the fest's famed Moose Toss, participants pitch dried moose droppings onto a table covered with numbers. The dropping that stays on the highest number wins.

The World Cow-Chip-Throwing Championships are held in April in Beaver, Oklahoma. Contestants fling dried cow patties, competing for distance. They usually sail rather like a frisbee.

But not everybody tosses cow dung. Some bet on it. Cow Patty Bingo is played every year during the August Festival in Slaton, Texas. Cow Patty Bingo starts by first marking off a parking lot into numbers to make a Texas-sized bingo card. Then, numbered tickets are sold at five dollars each. While the eager ticket holders surround the parking lot–bingo card, a cow is turned loose onto the card to wander where it will. Make that a *well-fed* cow. If the cow delivers a patty onto your number, you win a thousand dollars.

"Most years, the bingo goes pretty fast, sometimes within two minutes," says Darla Mason of the Slaton Chamber of Commerce. "Other years, the game can take up to two hours. We've learned to have several well-fed back-up cows in reserve."

A consolation prize of fifty dollars is paid in case the cow only waters on your number.

Several communities offer yearly duck races, but you won't hear any quacking because the participants are rubber ducks. Santa Monica, California, offers the Great Southern California Duck Race in May. The idea is to see how fast thirty thousand rubber ducks can float or bob from one end of the Santa Monica Pier to the other. The record for the one-third mile course is a leisurely 29:02. Race watchers sponsor a duck at five dollars each and proceeds go to a local hospital. And at the Third Annual Great Houston Duck Race, 20,438 rubber ducks floated down a popular downtown waterway known as Buffalo Bayou. Proceeds here also went to worthy causes.

All "horny toads" (*Genus Phrynosoma*) are welcome at the annual Horny Toad Race held in Needles, California, each September. Coaches try to coax their toads to hop out of a twenty-foot-diameter circle drawn in the dirt. Coaches can yell, pound the ground, or blow on the toads as long as the entrant is not touched.

The annual Chicken Show, held in Wayne, Nebraska, on the second Saturday in July, features a crowing contest for roosters, a free omelet feed for humans, and a chicken flying meet, fully sanctioned by the International Chicken Flying Association. You can enter your own chicken or rent one. Also featured: a most beautiful beak contest, chicken bingo games, and an egg drop for people wherein participants risk egg on the face by trying to catch bare-handed a raw egg dropped from a fully extended cherry picker. The National Cluck-Off selects the person with the most lifelike cluck and the most believable crow. Yet another contest offers prizes to the man and the woman who sport the most chicken-like legs on a human.

The annual Woolly Worm festival, held in October in Banner Elk, North Carolina, began because people there have traditionally used the black and brown stripes on the woolly worm *(Genus Archtiidae)* as an indicator of the severity of the approaching winter. However, nobody could ever say exactly *which* worm should be used for the annual prediction. Eventually, the town fathers decided the best way would be to hold a woolly worm race and read the stripes on the winner. One year, a vet attended the festival to make sure the competitors were racing free of drugs. Usually, there is a woolly worm first aid booth.

"There are all kinds of unknown facts about woolly worm health and nutrition, weight training, CPR, and gait analysis," says a chiropractor on the medical team.

The race course is arranged so the worms race three feet straight up dangling strings. The winner of each heat receives sixty dollars while the owner of the speediest worm overall collects five hundred dollars. A leading citizen then interprets the thirteen stripes on the winning worm and pronounces what type of winter approaches. The woolly worms have correctly predicted the onset and type of winter several times.

Traveling slower than even the slowest woolly worm are the entrants in The Great Snail Festival, held in southern California yearly in March.

" 'Pest' or 'pâté'? We never quite know how to promote the snail industry," says an event organizer. "We think it's best to leave the decision to the individual."

The Great American Bug Race, a running of cockroaches, matches about sixty roaches inside an eight-foot circle. The winner of the race, which tests the insects' speed and endurance, is the first to cross the border of the circle. The top award is $150. Training is difficult because most roaches tend to race in tight circles only.

Annually in Pearblossom, California, the Insects on Parade is held at Devil's Punchbowl County Park. Exotic creatures like an African millipede, the Madagascar hissing cockroach, Emperor and desert hairy scorpions, ironclad beetles, praying mantises, and a fifteen-year-old tarantula are displayed. Those who arrive with a clear plastic liter bottle can learn how to make a "bug condo."

If you're itching for mounds of fun, the annual FireAnt Festival, held since 1983 during the second weekend in October in Marshall, Texas, could be a good bet despite the painful sting for which the fire ant *(Solenopsis geminate)* is noted. Nine years ago, the town fathers noticed that nothing could make the fire ants and their pesky mounds go away entirely, so they decided to acknowledge their presence. At the most recent FireAnt shindig, a six-foot-tall Freddie FireAnt, his wife, who is billed as the fiery Elvira, and their offspring Sugar, greeted forty-five thousand visitors. Contests and events include the FireAnt Call and the FireAnt Roundup. The FireAnt Call, in which contestants use any instrument at hand, consists of an alarm call, a feeding call, and a mating call. The most recent winner used a kazoo to take top honors. The defending champion in the ant round-up was a man who corralled about 330 stray fire ants while suffering only 170 bites. The festival also features a chili cook-off in which entrants must certify *in writing* that their chili fixins contain at least one fire ant. The festivities are wrapped up with the FireAnt Stomp, which is not a mass attempt to squash ants, but an old-fashioned street dance.

Trying to raise the lowly image of all insects, the Insect Horror Film Festival is organized by entomologists yearly at the University of Iowa. The organizers want you to realize how badly insects have been treated, and that such creatures can be a genuine taste delight. For those with an adventuresome palate, treats like chocolate-covered grasshoppers, sauteed caterpillars, and garlic-flavored roasted larvae are available. The event also features a petting zoo that includes cockroaches, drone bees, tarantulas, giant walking sticks, water beetles, and dragonfly nymphs. The three-day festival features sci-fi horror films like *Them*, a 1950 film in which ordinary ants were transmogrified into seven-foot creatures by the first atomic bomb blasts. The organizers want to show how our fear of insects is largely unwarranted and that the majority of insects are actually beneficial to humankind.

One exception may be the pesky mosquito (Family Culicidae). Nonetheless, the Great Texas Mosquito Festival in Clute, Texas, honors the biting pests yearly. Opening ceremonies include events like "The Swatting of the First Mosquito," a one-mile run called the "Mosquito Chase," and the "Skeeter Beater" contest, which would be known elsewhere as a baby-crawling contest.

Other annual events centered around animals include festivals honoring: buffaloes, burros, cats, catfish, cows, crabs, dinosaurs, ordinary dogs, sled dogs, ducks, rabbits, horses, jumping frogs, gophers, raccoons, hogs, llamas, mules, pigs, rhinos, sharks, turtles, walruses, and humpback whales.

*   *   *

The Great American Beer Festival is held every October in Boulder, Colorado, for beer lovers *(Americanus Redneckus)*. Not only can you slake your thirst with hard-to-find brews like Pete's Wicked Ale or Sierra Nevada Bigfoot Barley Wine-Style Ale, you can rub shoulders with the burgeoning numbers of people who make home brew in kitchens and cellars. Microbrewers (who make less than fifteen thousand barrels a year) and brewpubs (establishments that make beer on the premises) are also on hand.

The celebrants in the Carry Nation Festival, held in September in Holly, Michigan, almost certainly eschew any festival that features any form of alcohol. The festival re-creates the ax-wielding barroom visits of Carry Nation, the famous Kansas City saloon smasher and temperance leader who lived from 1846 to 1911.

In 1987, newspaper columnist Les Mann, of Chadron, Nebraska, published a tribute to his beat-up three-quarter-ton pickup truck, a 1974-vintage vehicle he named Black Beauty. Mann wrote that his beloved Black Beauty was *THE* ugliest pickup anywhere. But outraged ugly-truck–owning readers wrote in, disputing Mann's claim. Thus, the annual Ugly Pickup Parade and Contest was first organized. A panel of expert judges selects the year's ugliest pickup in October. In 1989, the selection of an Ugly Pickup Queen was added. That queen now leads the parade while perched on the battered hood of the first pickup to register. Organizers say the accumulated mileage of the trucks entered in the most recent parade equaled two round trips to the moon. One entrant listed "ten trips around the planet" as the number of miles on his pickup's odometer.

Winning the Champion Ugly award was a vehicle known as Brown Sugar, a 1973 flatbed Ford with 160,224 miles on it. Graced with a plywood hood, Brown Sugar is used to haul firewood, honey, and beehives. Wradical Wrecker, second place co-winner, attracted a lot of attention because it carried a passenger, a character dressed as a Conehead. Booger, the other second place co-winner, is a yellow Ford with 133,000 miles on it that is used for general hauling. To enter, trucks must be at least ten years old and have a surface area that consists more of dents and rust than of chrome. Vehicles must also be street-legal, have a name worthy of an ugly pickup, and be able to negotiate the entire parade length (three city blocks) under its own, or the driver's, power. Judges may award extra points for especially eye-catching ugly features, like that plywood hood.

The parade organizers have banded together as the International Ugly Pickup Association and maintain the Ugly Pickup Hall of Fame where Black Beauty, the famed truck that started it all now rusts, er . . . *rests*.

Every Fourth of July, Barstow, California, also holds an Ugly Truck Contest. The most recent winning entry was spruced up by loading the vehicle's bed with an ironing board, a wooden horse, hubcaps, dozens of beer bottles, a king-sized bedspring, and various other junk, all tied down with a garden hose. Four bicycle frames were mounted upside down on the roof of the cab. Tool boxes were welded onto the front fenders while large squeegees replaced the windshield wipers. A motorcycle was attached to the front bumper. "They took one look and declared my truck the winner," says proud owner Eddie Parker of Barstow.

Yet another annual event for vehicles is the Salsa Fiesta on Wheels, held in June in Orange County, California. Many car enthusiasts equip their autos with hydraulic pumps that allow the fronts of the cars to jump into the air, so a car-hopping competition is held. The most recent winner was a self-described lowrider with a 1962 Chevy whose front end leaped a record forty-one inches into the air.

One car that rests squarely on terra firma is the vehicle that carried outlaws Bonnie Parker and Clyde Barrow during their two-year crime spree, and, finally, to their deaths in the early 1930s. Bonnie and Clyde met in Grapevine, Texas. So every year the holdup of the Grapevine Home Bank is reenacted by actors from the Depression Era Outlaws Living History Association at the Grapevine Main Street Days Festival. The bullet-riddled Bonnie and Clyde death car is usually on display.

Honoring all types and vintages of Detroit iron is Carhenge, a summer solstice celebration held on June 22 in a wheat field just north of Alliance, Nebraska. Geologist Jim Reinders built Carhenge in 1988 at a cost of twelve thousand dollars by planting twenty-six cars on end to form a replica of the famed Stonehenge in England. During the most recent observance, a twenty-seventh car was raised to form a capstone on the monument.

At the Museum of Flight in Seattle, Washington, the Great International Paper Airplane Contest provides a forum for armchair aviators to compete against other paper-airplane enthusiasts from around the world. Entrants sign up by mailing their paper plane to the museum, and compete in four categories: time aloft, distance, aerobics, and esthetic design.

Speaking of time aloft, an annual Bridge Day is celebrated in Fayetteville, West Virginia, by allowing parachutists to leap from the 876-foot-tall New River Gorge Bridge on the third Saturday in October. The average parachutist spends eight seconds in the air before experiencing a "water landing" or, if the river is low, touching down on a sandbar. If there's a lot of water in the river, rescue boats speed to the jumpers and pull them out. Despite all care, however, three have died because of parachute malfunctions since Bridge Day began in 1981, though one year, a jumper suffered a complete parachute malfunction and splashed down into the river with no break whatsoever in his fall. Rescuers found the man uninjured and fully conscious. He returned the following year to jump again, this time with a parachute that worked.

Every January, the Top That Tacky Banquet is held in Lancaster, Pennsylvania. The event is held close to Christmas so unwanted gifts can be entered, or worn, in various tacky competitions. Most recently, a statue of a female tropical island native, made of rope and wood, took top tacky honors because the breasts of the native were flashing red and green lights. Winning ensemble went to a woman wearing hot pink polyester stretch pants that were bell-bottomed, hip-hugging, and zippered in the rear. She wore a clashing floral top and multi-colored platform shoes. Some contestants complained, saying the woman nibbled on Cheese Whiz and Saltine crackers during the judging, thereby unfairly influencing the decision. Other items that have been worn include Cabbage Patch baby slippers, light-up plastic eyeglasses, Wonder Woman skates, and a tie, complete with shiny polyester scales, that looked like a long, skinny salmon. "It goes without saying that Graceland is like Mecca to us," said one of the organizers.

With a theme of "I'll Still Respect You in the Morning," Whittier College in Whittier, California, recently held the first annual Tacky Prom. A typical tackee arrived with her hair in curlers, unmatching nail colors, and a shark tooth necklace.

For three decades, the Headdress Ball has been held in San Bernardino, California. Some of the headdresses weigh up to thirty pounds, some are as tall as the models who wear them, and each requires a separate designer, builder, and sponsor. Some are made of aluminum tubing or screen wire, and require up to 150 hours of labor. One six-and-one-half-foot-wide hat flew its own flag and shot fireworks from its brim. Another hat revolved on the head of its wearer.

One of the most favorite yearly affairs of all is an event which was known for many years as "Stupid Pet Tricks." Hosted on the first Saturday in May, the Dallas Society for the Prevention of Cruelty to Animals now calls the contest "Precocious Pet Tricks." Standout contestants have included Maugham, a break-dancing cat who allowed his owner to spin him in furious circles on a slick plastic board while rock music played, and a Labrador retriever who could balance six dog biscuits on his nose, fling the stack skyward, and catch them all in his mouth. Snickers, a Chesapeake Bay retriever, once stole the show by retrieving cans of cold beer in his mouth for his owner from a distant cooler.

Another big hit with audiences was a beagle who leapt onto

the glass covering of a pinball machine and chased the ball as it ricocheted off the bumpers. Snoopy, a cat, washed his ears when his owner told him they were dirty. And a Pomeranian-spitz mixture howled along, more or less in tune, as her owner sang French opera.

The most recent Precocious Pet Tricks show included Bones, a French poodle who could go as limp as a dishrag on command and stay that way as its owner arranged the dog's body. But the pet that really brought the house down was a mongrel, part pit bull, who picked up a bowling ball in his mouth and carried it around the stage.

And if that isn't America at its finest, I don't know what is.

3
EVERY DAY A CELEBRATION:
HOLIDAYS YOU'VE NEVER HEARD OF

Near the Jamaican coast on April 9, 1731, Spanish pirates boarded a British ship, the *Rebecca*, and one of them used a saber to slice an ear off sailor Robert Jenkins. The pirates thoroughly plundered the ship and committed other outrages. Through the terror, Jenkins saved his severed ear, and displayed it seven years later while describing the atrocity to the House of Commons in London. The ensuing, but belated, hubbub caused Britain to declare war on Spain in October, 1739. The hostilities, known as "The War of Jenkins' Ear," lasted until 1743. While historians have recorded little else about Jenkins, they did mark well the day he lost his ear. Because, in England, April 9 is noted on calendars as Jenkins' Ear Day.

You may never have heard of Jenkins' Ear Day because Winston Churchill Day is also observed on April 9, the birthday of the former prime minister. That date is also celebrated in the United States as the day in 1945 when Churchill was named an honorary United States citizen.

If you look forward only to Christmas, Easter, July 4, New Year's, and maybe a couple of other holidays, you may not know what you're missing. It turns out that every day, week, and month is some sort of holiday or special occasion, somewhere. For all those who don't feel much cause to celebrate, here's ample proof otherwise.

For instance, there are three more reasons to celebrate January 1 in addition to its being plain old New Year's Day. It is also Pun Day, when the Pun Corps announces the previous year's ten best puns. The purpose? To salute the best punsters of the year and encourage wordplay, thereby combating illiteracy. The first day of the year is also New Year's Dishonor List Day, when overused words and incorrect phrases like "somewhat unique," "first time ever," and "safe sex" are put forward as candidates for banishment from the Queen's English. Z Day is also held on January 1 to provide recognition on the first day of the year for all persons and places whose names begin with the letter Z and consequently are always listed last.

January is marked as National Hobby Month, National Volunteer Blood Donor Month, and National Careers in Cosmetology Month. January 1 through 7 serves as both Weeks Week, a time set aside to call attention to all the weeks of special importance in the coming year, and Silent Records Week, honoring the thirtieth anniversary of the invention of a silent record issued by Soupy Sales and the 120-piece Hush Symphonic Band.

January 4 is General Tom Thumb's Day, because it remembers the birthday of perhaps the most famous midget in history. General Thumb was born in 1838; his real name was Charles Sherwood Stratton. His growth virtually stopped after his first year, but he reached a height of three feet, four inches, and a weight of seventy pounds. Stratton was discovered by circus owner P. T. Barnum in 1842 and became internationally known. He performed for Queen Victoria and other heads of state and was happily married to a woman somewhat shorter than he.

But much more important for this author is the fact that January 4 is also Trivia Day, celebrating those who know all sorts of useless facts.

National Joygerm Day is observed on January 8, when joygerms everywhere are encouraged to celebrate by hugging, smiling, grinning, and otherwise winning over grumps and grouches.

January 9 is Show and Tell Day at Work. The Big Kids' Show and Tell Society thinks it's only fair to extend school show and tell to working adults.

Sponsored by the Old Soldiers of Baker Street, the Sherlock Holmes Birthday Breakfast is held on January 11 at New York City's Algonquin Hotel. The breakfast is given in honor of Mrs. Hudson, the eternally busy landlady at 221B Baker Street.

January 12 is the birthday of Ira Hayes, one of six U.S. Marines who raised the American flag on Mount Suribachi on February 23, 1945, an event immortalized by Joe Rosenthal's famous photo. Hayes was born on a Pima Indian reservation in Arizona in 1922 and was a hero to everyone except himself. He was unable to cope with fame, became an alcoholic, and was arrested more than fifty times in thirteen years. In 1955, Hayes was found dead of exposure in freezing weather on the Sacaton Indian Reservation in Arizona.

A lighter time is January 13 through 19, which marks Cuckoo Dancing Week and honors the memory of Laurel and Hardy, whose theme song was "Cuckoos Dancing." The same week is also Man Watchers Week, when the ten most watchable men in the world are announced.

January 16 marks National Nothing Day, an event that will no doubt become more important to the reader as this chapter progresses. It was created by newspaperman Harold Pulman Coffin "to provide Americans with one national day when they can just sit . . . without celebrating, observing, or honoring anything."

The anniversary of the launching of the first nuclear-powered submarine, the *Nautilus*, is also January 16.

The next day marks the anniversary of the Palomares hydrogen bomb accident. On that date in 1966, an American B-52 had a mid-air collision, lost two hydrogen bombs, and scattered radioactive plutonium over farmland in Palomares, Spain.

The birthday of Englishman Thomas Crapper is on January

17. Born in 1837, he was the prime developer of the flush toilet mechanism as we know it today. The day is also Hat Day, which celebrates the multitude of head coverings worn around the world.

January 18 is Pooh Day, which celebrates the birthday of Alan Alexander Milne, the English author who is remembered for his books about Winnie the Pooh.

In Philadelphia, Big Ben's Birthday Bash—honoring the birthday of Benjamin Franklin—takes place on January 19 *and* 20.

King George V of England Death by Euthanasia Anniversary is on January 20. Fifty years after George's death in 1936, it was revealed that he had died at age seventy-one of a lethal injection given by his physician. George's final words were not "How is the Empire?" as was formerly believed, but "God damn you!"

January 20 marks National Clean Off Your Desk Day. Its purpose is to provide one day each year for every desk worker to see the top of his or her desk and prepare for the year's coming flood of paperwork. If your desk is already clean, that same day is also National Hugging Day.

National Handwriting Day, observed on January 23, also marks the birthday of John Hancock. The same day is National Pie Day, a day created to fete pie as an art form as well as a gastronomical delight.

One-Tooth Rhee Landing Day is observed on January 23 near government offices of all levels to mark the beginning of the "confusionist" branch of American bureaucracy. The sponsor of the day, the Pun Corps, says that One-Tooth Rhee, a mythical Korean inventor, came up with the custom of each government official wearing four hats so that contradictory sets of instructions could be given with each job title.

Clash Day is observed on January 23 in Rockford, Ohio. All employees at a nursing home there wear their most mismatched clothes to beat the mid-winter doldrums and to bring smiles to residents' faces.

January 24 is set aside as Spouses Day, when husbands and wives are encouraged to share jobs, roles, and responsibilities so they may better appreciate each other.

In Australia, January 26 is Australia Day because the first boatload of British convicts arrived at what is now Sydney on that date in 1788.

The anniversary of the Great Seal of the United States is on January 28. That same date is also National Kazoo Day, billed as a day to appreciate the kazoo as a musical instrument.

The Beatles' Last Public Appearance is observed on January 30. On that date in 1969, the Beatles played an impromptu concert on the roof of Apple Studios in London. The noontime gig was halted by bobbies, however, when dour neighbors complained of "noise."

As evidence of Congress's effectiveness, February is known as American Heart Month, American History Month, Black History Month, Creative Romance Month, Human Relations Month, Humpback Whale Awareness Month, and National Blah Buster Month, designed to provide comfort to all who suffer the winter blahs. The year's second month is also set aside as Return Shopping Carts to the Supermarket Month in Chicago. It's a time to return not only shopping carts but milk crates, bread trays, and ice cream baskets to stores to help keep down food price increases.

February 1 is Freedom Day, which celebrates the approval on that day in 1865 of the Thirteenth Amendment to the U.S. Constitution, abolishing slavery. The same day is also Robinson Crusoe Day, marking the anniversary of the rescue on that date in 1709 of Alexander Selkirk, a Scottish sailor who was put ashore in September, 1704, on Más a Tierra, one of the Juan Fernández islets in the South Seas.

National School Counseling Week is held February 2 through 8, while February 3 has been The Day the Music Died Day ever since the deaths of rock 'n' roll singers Buddy Holly, the Big Bopper, and Ritchie Valens in an airplane crash on that date in 1959.

Torture Abolition Day is also February 3, while February 3 through 7 is Dietary Managers Pride in Food Service Week.

On February 5, 1985, Hugo Vetere, mayor of Rome, and Chedli Klibi, mayor of Carthage, met at Tunis to sign a treaty officially ending the Third Punic War. The fighting started in the year 149 B.C. and stopped with the razing of Carthage in 146 B.C., resulting in 2,131 years of officially unended hostility. Ever since, February 5 has been celebrated as the ending anniversary of the longest war in history. A peace treaty was not inked back in 146 B.C. because there were no Carthaginians left to sign.

In the United States, February 5 is Weatherman's Day. It commemorates the birth of Dr. John Jeffries, a Boston physician born in 1744 and one of America's first weathermen.

February 6 is No Talk Day, to stress the importance of written communication skills in schools. Shortly after is the anniversary of the slogan "All the News That's Fit to Print." The slogan has appeared on page one of *The New York Times* daily since February 10, 1897.

February 9 is World Marriage Day, a special day to honor all marriages.

February 11 marks White Shirt Day. Blue-collar workers traditionally wear white shirts on this day to mark a union agreement made in 1937 at a General Motors plant following a forty-four-day, sit-down strike. Workers thought white shirts, rather than blue, would be more appropriate attire.

Margaret Ann Day is observed on February 13 for the thousands of women who are named Margaret Ann but who hate it. They can change their names to Margeaux for the day. It was started by a woman, Margaret Ann, who disliked being called Margaret or Marge. She thought Margeaux was exotic.

Ferris Wheel Day and Have a Heart Day are both celebrated on February 14. George Washington Gale Ferris, engineer and inventor, was born on that date in 1859. He built the first Ferris wheel, which was 250 feet in diameter and had 365 coaches, each capable of carrying forty passengers. The Ferris wheel was America's answer to the Eiffel Tower.

February 17 through 23 is International Friendship Week, National Retail Bakers Week, and National Engineers Week.

Elm Farm Ollie Day is observed on February 18, marking the first flight in an airplane by a dairy cow, in 1930. Elm Farm Ollie, a prize-winning guernsey, was taken aloft in a plane at the St. Louis International Air Exposition. The cow was milked while airborne, and some of the milk was parachuted to the crowd below.

Northern Hemisphere "Howdy-Hoo" Day is celebrated at high noon on February 20. Citizens are asked to go outdoors and yell "Howdy-Hoo" to chase away winter and make ready for spring, only a month away.

French Fry Friday, a day dedicated to the classic hamburger side dish, is on the fourth Friday in February.

March is reserved as Humorists are Artists Month, Mental Retardation Month, National Nutrition Month, Poetry Month, Red Cross Month, National Womens' History Month, Youth Art Month, and Music in Our Schools Month.

The second day of March is Peanut Butter Lovers' Day, which celebrates the 102nd anniversary of the invention of every kid's favorite sandwich spread. National Pig Day is the day before.

March 1 through 7 is Return Borrowed Books Week, while American Chocolate Week is observed March 16 through 21.

However, if fudge and candy bars don't do the trick, I Want You to Be Happy Day takes place on March 3, and is dedicated to reminding people to be thoughtful about others for whom things are not going well.

If you can get around to it, National Procrastination Week is scheduled March 2 through 8, and celebrated whenever. The idea is to promote the many benefits of relaxing by putting off until tomorrow, or the next day, things that need not be done today.

Old Inauguration Day is observed on March 4, when, from 1789 to 1933, newly-elected presidents took their oaths of office.

March 5 is the anniversary of Winston S. Churchill's "Iron Curtain" speech. In 1946 on that date, Churchill brought a new phrase into the language when he said: "From Stettin in the Baltic to Trieste in the Adriatic, an iron curtain has descended across the continent."

With more iron as a theme, Bang Clang Day on March 9 observes the first clash between ironclad warships, the USS *Monitor* and CSS *Merrimac*, which happened in 1862. The two ships fired cannons at each other point blank for a full day with inconclusive results. Sponsors urge people to celebrate Bang Clang Day by hitting cast-iron kettles with ball peen hammers and firing cap pistols while standing in waist-deep water.

March 9 is also Panic Day, a time set aside for those in a dither to run around the office, telling others they can't handle it anymore. However, relief is close at hand during Fun Mail Week, March 10 through 16. And if you can't get any relief with letters, March 11 through 17 is Shortwave Radio Week, a time to garner world news and opinions through that type of broadcasting.

In Hinckley, Ohio, March 15 is Buzzards' Day. According to tradition, this is when the buzzards, which are actually turkey vultures, return to Hinckley from their winter quarters in the Great Smoky Mountains.

However, not every holiday honors nature's creatures. March 16 is Saint Uhro's Day, celebrating the patron saint who drove the grasshoppers out of the vineyards in Finland and forever saved Finnish wines.

Fragrance Day and Snowman Burning Day are both celebrated on March 21. Staged by the Unicorn Hunters of Lake Superior State University in Sault Ste. Marie, Michigan, a snowman is burned in effigy after reading poems that hail winter's end. Frangrance Day celebrates the perfumes and natural odors all around us.

March 21 is marked as the Future Birthday of Captain James T. Kirk. The Riverside, Iowa, town council declared a spot behind the current barbershop to be the future birthplace of Captain James Kirk, commander of the starship *Enterprise*. Known as a future historical event, Kirk's birth is slated for March 21, 2228.

As if that weren't enough to celebrate, March 21 is also National Teenagers Day. National Goof-Off Day is the next day.

March 23 is Near Miss Day, recalling the day in 1989 when a mountain-sized asteroid zipped within five hundred thousand miles of earth, creating a near miss, in astronomical terms at least.

Sponsored by the Wellness Permission League, March 26 is Make Up Your Own Holiday Day. The League says you may name the day for whatever you wish.

If you're born with a strange name, or a name you don't care for, March 27 is observed as National Joe Day. On that day, you can be known as Joe or Joan.

Doctors Day has been observed on March 30 since 1933, in honor of the first use of ether, during surgery in 1842 by Dr. Crawford W. Long. The red carnation has been named official flower of Doctors Day.

I Am in Control Day is also March 30. The occasion commemorates the date in 1980 when President Ronald Reagan was undergoing surgery after being shot by a would-be assassin. Secretary of State Alexander Haig announced to the American public on TV: "As of now, I am in control here in the White House."

March ends with the 31st, set aside for Bunsen Burner Day.

*   *   *

April marks Knuckles Down Month, a time to keep alive the tradition of playing marbles. The month is also reserved as International Guitar Month, National Humor Month, Holy Humor Month, Month of the Young Child, National Anxiety Month, National Cable Month, and National Woodworking Month. It is also the month when the International Twit Award is given. Any celebrity who is felt to possess the most tiresome wit (twit) is eligible.

Egg Salad Week, dedicated to the most common ultimate use of Easter eggs, is reserved for April 1 through 7. The same week is Publicity Stunt Week. It was started forty years ago during a slow business time by John Falk, a New York City press agent. Because he temporarily had no clients, Falk decided to publicize himself. Falk wrote to Buckingham Palace in London and claimed he was the only living descendant of Viscount Falkland, the person who discovered the Falkland Islands, a group of two hundred islands several hundred miles off the coast of southern Argentina. Falk claimed the viscount had willed the islands not to Her Majesty but to his heirs. And because John Falk was the last of the line, he wanted immediate control. (The story was farfetched because the Falklands were discovered in 1592 by John Davis and named for Falkland, a treasurer of the British Navy, in 1690.) The claim made the front page of the London *Times* for several days but brought Falk neither islands nor clients.

Armenian Appreciation Day is celebrated on April 3. Honored are Americans like Paul Boonian, who became mythologized as Paul Bunyan.

April 4 through 10 sees misanthropes everywhere enjoying Hate Week, a time that recognizes the anniversary of the week the fictional character Winston Smith started his secret diary in the book *1984* by penning the words, "Down With Big Brother!" For more gentle souls, the same week is also National Reading a Road Map Day, a time to promote map reading as an enjoyable pastime.

Sorry, Charlie Day is April 4 and honors the number-one loser, Charlie the Tuna, who has been turned down for thirty years but keeps on trying anyhow. The day also recognizes anyone else who has been rejected and lived through it.

Encourage a Beginning Writer Day is on April 10, which is the birthday of Joseph Pulitzer.

April 18 is reserved as Pet Owners' Independence Day. Because many pets just sleep all day and never even take out the garbage, the Wellness Permission League thinks cat and dog owners should take the day off from work and send their pets in their place.

The Grange, the fraternal, social, and political organization that represents one million farmers and their families in thirty-seven states, marks Grange Week from April 19 through 25. The same week is Professional Secretaries Week, and Reading Is Fun Week.

April 4 is set aside at the University of Colorado at Boulder as Alfred G. Packer Day, for America's only convicted cannibal. In 1873 only Packer returned from a journey in which six men had been stranded by deep winter snows. Packer aroused suspicion because he looked well-fed while his five companions had reportedly starved to death. It was soon discovered that Packer had killed, and eaten, the other five.

Although the incident took place two hundred miles away, the student body at the University of Colorado voted in 1968 to officially name its cafeteria the Alfred G. Packer Cafeteria as a commentary on the food. Sponsored by the university's food service branch, April 4 is just before final exams and is a day of frivolity on the campus.

Matanzas Mule Day is marked on April 27. On that date in 1898, the U.S. Navy bombarded Matanzas, Cuba, during the Spanish-American War, where it was widely reported that the only casualty was a mule.

A more kindly holiday is April 28, when Kiss Your Mate Day is celebrated. April 30 is National Honesty Day.

                       *   *   *

May honors American Bike Month, Better Sleep Month, Correct Posture Month, Foot Health Month, Freedom Shrine Month, Touring Theater Month, National Good Car Keeping Month, National Photo Month, Senior Citizens Month, National Duckling Month, and Revise Your Work Schedule Month. That's a time to consider nontraditional work schedules like flex-time and work sharing. In 1991, May 1 through 31 was set aside to honor the golden anniversary of Cheerios.

Lumpy Rug Day is celebrated on May 3. Its purpose is to tease bigots for shoving unwanted facts under the rug. The same date starts the celebration of International Tuba Week.

No Socks Day is observed on May 8. The sponsors think giving up socks for a day will mean a little less laundry and perhaps a better environment. May 12 is both Kite Day and Mother Ocean Day.

Few observe the anniversary of the National Anthem Memorizing Resolution, May 19. In 1932, Congressman Claude A. Fuller introduced a bill requiring all United States civil servants to show they had memorized the words to the Star Spangled Banner. The bill later died in committee.

So we won't forget the bounty of food, many special times during the year are set aside to honor gastronomical delights.

For instance, the pickle, often billed as the world's most humorous vegetable, seemingly heads the list of food holidays. There is a Pickle Month, an International Pickle Week, Shape Up With Pickles Time, Snack-a-Pickle Time, Pickled Peppers Week, and, finally, Holidays Are Pickle Days, whose purpose is to promote the pickle as a special dish for holidays from Thanksgiving all the way to New Year's Day.

Other food holidays during the year include a Pizza Week and Month, Pancake Week, National Oatmeal Month, National Gingerbread Day, Corn Month, National Egg Month, Peach Month, National Cherry Month, Macadamia Nut Month,

Homemade Bread Day, Meat Month, and Prune Breakfast Month.

Even snacks have their own special time. There are an Ice Cream Day and Month, Pecan Day, Dr. Cookie Week, a Peanut Month and Day, National Popcorn Day, National Popcorn Poppin' Month, Bubble Gum Week, and National Pie Day.

To wash it all down are: National Applejack Month, American Beer Week, and National Homebrew Days.

First observed in 1938 as a fund-raiser for the Salvation Army, Donut Days are June 5 and 6 in Chicago.

If you've observed the majority of these holidays, you may want to skip ahead on your calendar and flag National Eating Disorders Week, November 21 through 28, in red ink.

Besides Donut Days, the month of June celebrates Cancer in the Sun Month, to make people aware of the dangers of sunshine to the skin, Gay and Lesbian History month, National Adopt-a-Cat Month, National Rose Month, National Tennis Month, and National Zoo and Aquarium Month.

Marilyn Monroe's birthday, June 1, 1926, is shared with the Plymouth Plantation Earthquake anniversary. The first temblor recorded in America was described on June 1, 1638, by Governor William Bradford, who wrote: ". . . ye earth shooke with ye violence as (men) could not stand without catching hold of ye posts. But ye violence last not long. After about halfe an hour or less, came another noyse & shaking, but neither so loud nor strong as ye former, but quickly passed over, and so it ceased."

June 2 is Yell "Fudge" at the Cobras in North America Day. According to the holiday's sponsors, the word "Fudge" makes cobras gag and slither away.

The anniversary of the first free flight by a woman, Marie Thimble, of Lyon, France, is marked on June 2. On that date in 1784, Marie became the first woman to fly in an unattached balloon.

June 6 is National Sure You Can Travel Day to encourage

the handicapped to learn all about the possibility of traveling. The same day is also National Yo-yo Day, commemorating the birth of Donald F. Duncan, the toy's inventor, in 1892.

The Kentucky Historical Society celebrates June 7 as Boone Day, after the day Daniel Boone first sighted the land that would become Kentucky, in 1767.

If you tend to keep a lot of things up in the air, be sure and circle June 13 on your calendar. It's National Juggling Day. Hug Holidays take place June 15 through 22. Their purpose is to express appreciation of others through any acceptable form, but especially through a simple hug.

World Sauntering Day is June 19. The idea is to revive the lost art of Victorian sauntering while discouraging jogging, fast walking, trotting, or other forms of non-leisurely locomotion.

June 24 is the anniversary of the first flying saucer sighting over Mount Rainier, Washington, in 1947.

A holiday known as Juneteenth is celebrated on June 19 in Texas and some other parts of the Deep South. It marks the day in 1865 when Union general Gordon Granger proclaimed all slaves in Texas free men and women.

Happy Birthday to Happy Birthday to You is on June 27. That melody, composed by Mildred J. Hill on that date in 1859, is considered to be the world's most frequently sung song.

Each July is Hitchhiking Month, Anti-Boredom Month, National Parks and Recreation Month, National Picnic Month, and Read an Almanac Month, the sponsors of which want you to know that almanacs aren't just for farmers anymore.

Dog Days begin on July 3 and last through August 15. The period is so named because ancient Romans believed the heat of the season was caused when Sirius, the Dog Star, rose about the same time as the sun. Moreover, the ancients sacrificed a brown dog to the Dog Star when it first appeared, hoping to appease the beastly rage of Sirius. Air Conditioning Days are marked for the same period in the Northern Hemisphere; however, no dogs are sacrificed.

In addition to our nation's birth, July 4 is American Redneck Day, National Country Music Day, Hillbilly Day, and Ann Landers's birthday.

Bowdler's Day is marked on July 11. Dr. Thomas Bowdler, a prudish English physician, removed from the works of Shakespeare all the words he thought indecent or impious and reissued the works in ten "family" volumes on that date in 1818. Ever since, "bowdlerizing" has been the word for self-righteous expurgation.

National Nude Days, which are seldom bowdlerized, are July 11 and 12. The holiday promotes acceptance of the body.

Atomic Bomb Day is on July 16. At 5:30 A.M. on that date in 1945 at Alamagordo Air Base, 120 miles south of Albuquerque, New Mexico, the first atomic bomb was exploded.

Spooner Day is marked on July 21. The day is named for the Reverend William Archibald Spooner, whose frequent slips of the tongue—"blushing crow," instead of crushing blow, "tongues of soil," instead of sins of toil, "half moon fish," instead of half-formed wish, and so on—led to the word spoonerism.

In Germany, Rat-Catchers Day is on July 22 and honors the twelfth-century Pied Piper of Hamelin, as well as modern-day pest exterminators.

The birthday of the first test-tube baby, Louise Brown, born in 1978, is celebrated on July 25. Many scientists have pointed out that Louise is actually a Petri dish baby, but "test-tube" seems to have stuck.

July 27 marks Take Your House Plants for a Walk Day. The day's sponsors think your plants will become more healthy from knowing their environment.

Special days in August begin with International Clown Week, from the 1st through the 7th. Beauty Queen Week shares the spotlight during the same dates. August is also National Water Quality Month and Romance Awareness Month.

On August 3, 1492, one-half hour before sunrise, Christopher Columbus set sail from Palos, Spain, for what he thought was China.

Lizzie Borden Liberation Day is August 4. Lizzie Borden was charged with and acquitted of killing her father and stepmother with an ax on August 4, 1892. But the thirty-two-year-old spinster remained guilty in the public mind anyhow. Friends of Lizzie Borden celebrate the day to help free her name. Appropriately enough, that day is also Friendship Day.

Presidential Joke Day is August 11. It commemorates the day in 1984 when President Ronald Reagan was asked to give a voice test on what he thought was a dead microphone but instead broadcast live: "My fellow Americans, I am pleased to tell you I just signed legislation which outlaws Russia forever. The bombing begins in five minutes." August 11 is also the beginning of Beatles National Apple Week, celebrating the creation in 1965 of the Apple Recording Label.

International Left-Handers Day is on August 13.

August 15 is National Relaxation Day, the Anniversary of Woodstock, and Virginia Dare Day. Virginia was the first child born to English parents in the New World, on August 15, 1587.

Be Kind to Humankind Week, August 25 through 31, has a gentle theme for each day of the week. There are: Sacrifice Our Wants for Others' Needs Sunday; Motorists Consideration Monday; Touch a Heart Tuesday; Willing to Lend a Hand Wednesday; Thoughtful Thursday; Favors Granted Friday; and Be Compassionate Saturday.

August 29 is According to Hoyle Day, a time that reminds people to play poker, and everything else, by the rules.

The last day of August is Capital Day, a time to honor American savers and investors who directly, or indirectly, provide funds for the economy to grow.

*   *   *

September of each year is Be Kind to Editors and Writers Month, a time for journalists to show uncommon courtesy to each other. It is also Cable TV Month, National Courtesy Month, National Piano Month, and International Gay Square Dance Month.

September 1 is Emma M. Nutt Day. It honors the first woman telephone operator who started her job in Boston on this day in 1878 and stuck with it for thirty-three years.

September 2 through 5 observes the Great Fire of London Anniversary in England. That fire, generally credited with bringing about the current system of fire insurance, began on September 2, 1666, and burned for three days, destroying most of the city and more than thirteen thousand homes.

Newspaper Carrier Day, September 4, honors the anniversary of the hiring of the first newsboy in the United States. He was ten-year-old Barnie Flauerty, who answered an ad in the *New York Sun* in 1883.

An event young Barnie would never, never have celebrated is Be Late for Something Day on September 5. Sponsored by the Procrastinators' Club, the idea is to gain a breather from the stress caused by the constant pressure to be on time. If you do celebrate that day, be prepared for National Boss/Employee Exchange Day on the 14th and Swap Ideas Day on the 10th.

If by now you're overwhelmed by so many specialized occasions, don't look to this author for responsibility; simply plan ahead for March 13—National Blame Somebody Else Day.

September 16 is Stay Away from Seattle Day, which the sponsor hopes will be observed worldwide. The purpose is to give "America's best place to live a break from the influx of people moving there."

If you've only been able to conceive of one thing, then September 25, National One-Hit Wonder Day, may be for you. Officially, the day commemorates anyone who has had only one rock 'n' roll hit.

*   *   *

When October rolls around, don't forget it's International Microwave Month, Consumer Information Month, National Kitchen and Bath Month, Liver Awareness Month, Clock Month, Adopt-a-Dog Month, and National Sarcastics Awareness Month, the purpose of which is to help people understand the positive as well as the negative aspects of sarcasm.

October 2 is the birthday of cartoon characters Charlie Brown and Snoopy, who are said to be forty-two years old but don't look a day over six. It is also Phineas Fogg's Wager Day According to Jules Verne. On that day in 1872, Fogg and another British gent made a bet of twenty thousand pounds that sent Fogg on a journey around the world in eighty days.

Ten-Four Day is observed on the fourth day of the tenth month in recognition of radio operators everywhere, who use the code, "10-4," as an affirmative reply.

October 12 marks International Moment of Frustration Scream Day. The Low Threshold League asks all citizens of the world to go outside at 1200 hours Greenwich time and scream for thirty seconds. National Pet Peeve Week starts on this day and lasts until October 19. The idea is make others aware of all the little things in life they find so annoying in hopes of changing at least a few.

If your frustration is caused by a lack of hair, October 14 is Be Bald and Free Day. The day, to "go shiny and be proud," is for those who are bald and wear a toupee. The same day is National Frump Day. National Grouch Day is October 15. The following day is National Boss Day.

Doomsayers will want to note October 22, which is World's End Day, the date in 1844 when a religious leader, William Miller, decided the world would end. Miller and all his followers sold their possessions and retreated to high ground.

Horseless Carriage Day and Mule Day are both on October 26. Mother-in-Law Day falls on October 27.

*   *   *

Observed in England, Australia, and New Zealand, November 4 marks Mischief Night, a time for bonfires and firecrackers to commemorate the failure of Guy Fawkes's plot to blow up England's Houses of Parliament in 1605.

In the United States, the first Saturday in November marks Sadie Hawkins Day, when women and girls are encouraged to invite the men or boys of their choice on a date. The tradition was established in the town of Dogpatch in the *Li'l Abner* comic strip drawn by Al Capp when strong mountain gals chased, caught, and hog-tied their guys.

November 6 is Saxophone Day; November 7, Abet and Aid a Punster Day; November 14, Operating Room Nurse Day; November 17, Homemade Bread Day; and November 19, Have a Bad Day Day. That's a day for people who are filled with revulsion at being endlessly told to "Have a nice day." Others will enjoy November 21, World Hello Day. The idea is to greet— *nicely*—at least ten new people that day.

November 27 is You're Welcomegiving Day, the sole purpose of which is to create a four-day weekend beginning with Thanksgiving. November 30 is marked as Stay Home Because You're Well Day, a time to call in "well" to work instead of faking an illness.

Bingo's Birthday is celebrated for the entire month of December because the game's inventor, Edwin S. Lowe, got the idea one December in 1926 while traveling in Georgia where a similar French import, Beno, was played. But Lowe could never remember the exact day he saw Beno. When Lowe's new game was first tried, one player called out "Bingo" instead of "Beno" and the name stuck. Today, Bingo raises about $5 billion yearly for charity. Underdog Day is on the 18th; its purpose is to salute all the underdogs and unsung heroes who contribute so much to more renowned, number-one people. The 21st is Humbug Day, which allots everybody a total of twelve humbugs to vent holiday frustrations. The same day, which has the longest night of the year, is National Flashlight Day, when a flashlight is most needed. December 21 is also Phineas Fogg Wins a Wager Day. Fogg completed the eighty-day journey around the world with one second to spare.

National Whiner's Day, December 26, is dedicated to those who complain endlessly as they return Christmas gifts in crowded stores.

The final day of the year is set aside as Make Up Your Mind Day and You're All Done Day, the purposes of which are to make a decision (particularly for those who have a hard time making up their minds), and to savor the satisfaction of tasks completed, respectively.

Ending the year is a Noon Year's Eve party in Albuquerque, New Mexico, for early risers who have difficulty staying awake until midnight. It is sponsored by a morning radio show host, who leads the toast of "Happy Noon Year!"

No doubt you're wondering how some of these commemorative dates ever came to be recognized. The originator in many cases is our own government. Almost every day throughout the year in Congress, a lawmaker introduces a bill to mark a special day, week, month, year, or decade. Although some legislators want to end the practice—each bill costs about two thousand dollars just to consider—our representatives spend a lot of time considering which days or periods should be marked special.

According to Congressman Dave McCurdy, Democrat of Oklahoma, 30 percent of the bills passed by the 101st Congress were for special dates of commemoration. "Of 650 laws passed, 195 were commemorative," Congressman McCurdy says.

Another lawmaker, Claudine Schneider of Rhode Island, figured that printing and staff time for considering and passing commemorative events costs taxpayers $387,000 yearly. Others have estimated the annual cost at $500,000.

*   *   *

If some of the above official holidays seem unusual, it's worth taking a look at other holidays that have been proposed but rejected. So here is a partial list of bills that have been heard and debated on the floor of Congress, but not passed into law:

Polish Constitution Day, National Play-It-Safe Month, Purple Heart Month, Duck Stamp Week, Medical Transcriptionist Week, Multi-Housing Laundry Industry Week, National Sewing Week, National Jukebox Week, Recovery Room Nurses Day, National Snowmobiling Month, Jogging Day, Polish-American Heritage Month, National Flowers by Wire Day, National Boat Hunters Week, National Cheeseburger Week, Fraternal Insurance Counselor of the Month, National Home Remodeling Month, National Dollhouse and Miniature Week, Scuba Week, National Cosmetology Month, Elvis Presley Day, National Junior Bowling Championship Week, International Ventriloqists Week, National Prom/Graduation Day, Old Cars Week, National Ceramic Tile Industry Recognition Week, National Twins Day, American Beer Week, Steamboat Willie Recognition Day, 25th Anniversary of the movie *It's a Mad, Mad, Mad, Mad World*, National Fishing Week, National Wrestling Day, National Brick Week, National Day of Recognition of the Polish Armed Forces.

Talk about missed opportunities! But then, it's nice to know that Congress hasn't wasted its time on unimportant matters.

4
OFF-THE-WALL MUSEUMS

An elementary school teacher once took her class to visit a museum of natural history and found the children were delighted with it. After the trip, one excited child rushed home and blurted to his mother: "Guess what, Mom? The teacher took us to a dead circus today!"

If a deceased and stuffed menagerie struck that boy as odd, he would certainly have greater trouble making sense out of some of America's less traditional museums.

For instance, the Mustard Museum in Mount Horeb, Wisconsin, has over one thousand unusual brands on display. Among the museum's collection of pristine jars are the following flavors: golden ginger, Kerala curry, toasted garlic and raspberry vinegar, thyme, jalapeno, caraway, green chili, tangy sage, beer and orange ginger, barley, and a brand containing whiskey. There are fads even in the mustard world, so recent acquisitions include fruit-flavored mustards made with cherries, apricots, figs, peaches, lemons, and raspberries.

The Mount Horeb Mustard Museum also issues its own label. Owner, curator, and self-proclaimed mustard king Barry Levenson explains how the label was named: "When I asked my wife Pat what she thought about our chances of launching a mustard, she said the scheme had two chances. So, I named my mustards accordingly." Thus inspired, Levenson's labels now read: "Your chances of finding a better mustard are . . . Slimm and Nunne."

The museum issues an occasional newsletter, which contains ratings of new mustards, thank-you notes to contributors for adding to the burgeoning collection, recipes for dishes like Fish and Mustard, Green Beans and Mustard Sauce, and Mustard Spice Cake. It also carries articles about how mustard has been used in medicine. Besides the traditional mustard plaster, there have been preparations like Begy's True Mustarine, which was used to relieve soreness caused by overexertion. The mustard foot bath was once the treatment of choice for a condition known as the "chilblains"—soreness caused by exposure of the feet to cold.

Mustard memorabilia include a framed piece of sheet music for "Too Much Mustard," a song by Cecil Macklin. A tape of it plays while visitors browse through the museum. Also on view are a Johnson & Johnson Mustard Plaster tin donated by a physician, and a card from the game Clue, depicting the character Colonel Mustard, the patron saint of the museum.

"To supplement our own line of mustard, I've been developing a few new brands for us out-of-control mustard fanatics," Levenson says. "One is Happy Trails Thorazine Mustard, and for a more general audience, our bland but cheery Mellow Yellow Valium Mustard."

The Campbell Museum at Campbell Place in Camden, New Jersey, features soup tureens, bowls, and ladles, dating from 500 B.C. Most were imported into America from 1700 to 1840. Favorites include soup plates once owned by Russia's Czar Alexander II. The 350-piece collection includes a variety of soup tureens shaped like a swan, a ship, a tub of writhing fish, a melon, a bull's head, a head of lettuce, and one like a head of cauliflower. One is made of porcelain crustaceans and seaweeds. Many of the ornate tureens were crafted by master silversmiths; others are rare porcelains. One tureen is topped with a massive, detailed silver sculpture showing four hounds attacking a bear. Nobody at the Campbell Museum, however, has speculated on what our ancestors would have thought about dishing up soup from throw-away tin cans.

The Nut Museum in Old Lyme, Connecticut, is located on the ground floor of Elizabeth Tashijian's sixteen-room Victorian mansion. Since its opening in 1972, thousands have looked at her collection of rare nutcrackers, including one ten-foot-long model. You can also see a walnut on which is painted a miniature wedding scene; a whopping thirty-five pound double coconut, alleged to be the world's largest; hickory nutshell earrings; nut masks; and other bits of artistic nuttery. Because Curator Tashijian also has a theory that humankind descended not from the ape, but from the nut, plans are in the works for a nut theme park, something like Disneyland. The park would have a monument to the Egyptian sky goddess, Nut.

The Nut Museum is for true aficionados because admission is three dollars and one of any type of nut. (One fast-thinking tourist tried to pass off his wife as the nut, but his offer was rejected.) Ms. Tashijian, a self-proclaimed "nut visionary," says she fell in love with nuts as a child and painted many nut still lifes. So she collected nuts long before opening her museum.

The Phillips Mushroom Museum is located in Kennett Square, Pennsylvania, a community that bills itself as The Mushroom Capital of the World. Opened in 1972 because visitors' many questions about the edible fungi were simply, well, *mushrooming*, the museum traces the beginning of commercial mushroom growing. Ancient Egyptian kings believed that mushroom-eating led to immortality. During the times of the ancient Greeks and Romans, it was thought that mushrooms gave warriors great strength. The French—who knew the delicacy as a *mousseron*—passed to the English the secrets of commercially grown mushrooms, which arrived in America about 1896. A ten-minute film at the Mushroom Museum details the stages of mushroom development. While there are about thirty-eight thousand varieties of mushrooms, only *Agaricus bisporus* is cultivated commercially. According to the Phillips family, owners of the Mushroom Museum, mushroom growing is as difficult as growing orchids, since mushrooms like cold, shun sunlight, and are finicky about temperature and humidity. The museum has living displays of exotic mushrooms like the Asian Shiitake (six dollars a pound), the Portabella, the Japanese Enokitake or Enoki, the Cremini, and the Roman, which also may be known as brown or Italian mushrooms. There is an Oyster mushroom which looks like a large leaf.

The Potato Museum in Blackfoot, Idaho, offers such assorted potato lore as a two-thousand-year-old potato from Peru (where a potato god was worshipped) and the world's largest potato chip.

The Chicken Museum in Corbin, Kentucky, sits in a restaurant once operated by Harlan Sanders—better known as Colonel Sanders—in 1940. The museum has 1940-era conveniences like a Vulcan oven and the Hobard dishwasher used by the Colonel. Sanders was made an honorary Kentucky Colonel in recognition of his contributions to the state's cuisine, and he is often credited with giving birth to the fast-food era.

For some real fun, the Tupperware Museum of Historic Food Containers in Orlando, Florida, is worth a visit. On display are 233 historical containers made from all types of materials. One container dates back to four thousand B.C.

Two of America's favorite beverages, Coca-Cola and Dr. Pepper, each have a museum.

The Dr. Pepper Museum and Free Enterprise Institute in Waco, Texas, features a working soda fountain commemorating the Waco drugstore where Charles Alderton, a young doctor, created Dr. Pepper in 1885. Other displays include turn-of-the-century bottles labeled: "We pay for evidence convicting thieves for refilling our bottles." But the problem found solution in the early 1920s when bottlers began embossing their names on the bottles.

The three-story Coca-Cola Museum in Atlanta, Georgia, shows one of two existing prototype bottles first used for Coke 104 years ago. In the Coca-Cola showplace, there are a 1930-era drugstore soda fountain, docents decked out in bright red uniforms, and a jukebox that plays a list of Coca-Cola's "fountain favorites"—songs like "Sweet Coca-Cola Blush," "My Coca-Cola Bride," "Coca-Cola Joe," "Coca-Cola Waltz," and "When the Dodo Bird is Singing in the Coca-Cola Tree." A theater in the museum screens a nineteen-minute show of Coke TV commercials through four decades. The showplace also dishes up handy Coke trivia. For instance, about seven thousand soft drinks from the company are drained every second worldwide. The longest Coca-Cola distribution route is in Australia. To reach the isolated areas of Karratha and Port Hedland, a driver travels 1,093 miles from Perth, West Australia. The first painted, outdoor sign advertising Coke—done in 1894 in Cartersville, Georgia—still exists. And finally, if all the Coca-Cola ever produced were put in regular-size bottles and distributed to every person in the world, everybody on earth would have a stock of 767 bottles.

If you cotton to stronger beverages, the Oscar Getz Museum of Whiskey History in Bardstown, Kentucky, offers a backward glance at the last two hundred years of whiskey making. Kentucky bourbon, according to the museum, got its start in 1789 when the Reverend Elijah Craig accidentally burned some white oak barrels he intended to fill with corn whiskey at his distillery. Some of the barrels were scorched inside but the thrifty Craig used them anyway. The charred wood changed the clear corn whiskey into the mellower amber-colored drink that eventually helped make Kentucky famous. Whiskey drinkers clamored for more, and, by the mid-1850s, all Kentucky whiskey makers were charring their barrels.

The museum offers whiskey history viewed from pre-Colonial times, through Carry Nation, on through Prohibition and to the present. On display are stills, a Victorian bar, novelty whiskey containers (many are shaped like log cabins), antique bottles, whiskey jugs, and some of those barrels that were accidentally scorched. One bottle was produced in 1854 by F. G. Booz, a Philadelphia liquor dealer whose name would forevermore be synonymous with all alcoholic drinks. The museum also features an unopened collection of 157 Prohibition-era "medicinal liquor" bottles, dating from 1920 to 1933. That was booze you could only get with a doctor's prescription. You can also see a diorama of Abraham Lincoln's general store, which eventually became a tavern, and his 1833 liquor license.

"We wanted to put the fun back in garbage," says Jim Lochmiller, spokesman for a garbage museum in San Jose, California. "This is a place where talking trash is just good, clean fun."

The museum is officially known as the Browning-Ferris Industries Education Center. Located next to a garbage dump, a permanent collection of half-eaten pizzas, beer can empties, plastic bags, food scraps, broken toys, fast food wrappers, and empty product boxes is part of the recycling facility.

The first thing museum-goers see is the "Wall of Garbage," a hundred-foot-long, twenty-foot-high collection of junk, representing the garbage thrown away by one person every six years, or by the entire United States every second. All the items are authentic garbage which has been sterilized; vegetable matter has been carefully preserved. One of the museum's hands-on attractions is a laser wand that will pinpoint any item in the Wall with a beam. Next, you see a readout telling if that particular piece of junk is recyclable. Another exhibit shows what happens to glass bottles, metal cans, and paper products when they are properly recycled and transmogrified into new products.

Tidbits of garbage trivia from around the world are also presented. For instance, in Japan, old newspapers can be exchanged for toilet paper. Or, each recycled beverage can contains enough energy to power a TV set for three years.

The Trash Museum in Lyndhurst, New Jersey, shows visitors the amount of trash we toss out by displaying a simulated landfill. Although odor-free, the floor-to-ceiling exhibit is real trash, and includes Christmas tree lights, rusted car parts, toys, bottles, and an old washing machine.

Another type of junk—junk mail—is being collected for a museum in Los Angeles. Warren Meyer, owner of Meyer & Son Mailhouse, one of the nation's largest mailers of bulk material, is building the Junk Mail Museum in Studio City, California. Even if your name is not "Occupant" or "Resident," you'll want to read examples of Ronald Reagan fund-raising letters, ads for the 1984 Olympics, oversized postcards advertising wristwatches, avant-garde museum mailers, and a rambling letter from a man who swears junk mail killed his uncle. The man's alleged proof was that when the body of his uncle was found, the corpse was surrounded by piles of unsolicited mail stacked to the ceiling of his home. The writer claimed that the junk mail prevented his uncle from finding important mail, ultimately leading to his demise. Also on display will be examples of computerized goofs ("Dear Mr. Washington Post") and envelopes designed so that a check appears to be inside. Curator Warren Meyer is still searching for an example of the junk mailings of P. T. Barnum from the turn of the century.

The TV & Toy Museum in Orlando, Florida, offers two thousand bits of treasure from television's storied past. You'll find Twiggy eyelashes, Oscar Mayer wiener whistles, and a Laugh-In lunch box. By chance, the museum is located in a shopping center where former televangelists Jim and Tammy Faye

Bakker once held services. Seven years ago, museum owners Joane and Kirk Holcomb started their collection of TV memorabilia with a Charlie the Tuna doll. Soon, their spare room was filled with TV tidbits so they moved it all to larger quarters. Typical items on hand include a Voyage to the Bottom of the Sea lunch box, Bullwinkle and Rocky Presto Sparkle paint sets, Gidget board games, and a Flying Nun punch out paper doll. Clips of old shows run in a back room on vintage television sets.

Some of these collectibles that are dearest to the Holcombs' hearts are an Easter egg once autographed by actor Eddie Albert and twenty-five items signed by Soupy Sales. The museum also offers little-known facts about television personalities. For instance, not many know that Charles Manson once tried out for The Monkees or that the Pillsbury Dough Boy has a brother named Popper, a baby sibling (Bun-Bun, of undetermined gender), and a cat named Biscuit. Moreover, Lawrence Welk played not only the accordion but the spoons. The museum's most prized acquisition is the Beatles collection, which features an official wig, a Beverly Hillbilly's windup car, a Tom Corbett Space Cadet, and Soupy Sales lunch boxes.

According to Ted Hake's "Guide to TV Collectibles," a 1960s Flintstones lunch box is worth two hundred dollars, while Hopalong Cassidy roller skates can fetch three hundred dollars.

The World Kite Museum and Hall of Fame in Long Beach, Washington, says it is the only museum in America devoted to kites and their handlers. The museum is associated with an international kite festival, which most recently flew the world's largest kite, as big as a ten-story building. That kite requires a crew of ten to fly it. The Hall of Fame honors pioneers like Lawrence Hargraves, the English inventor who developed the camber-wing box kite in 1893, which led to the evolution of the wing for use in powered flight.

If your toy of choice is the marble, the American Toy Marble Museum in Akron, Ohio, may be for you. Though Akron is more commonly associated with tires, the museum claims the town is actually "The Toy Marble Capital of the World" because marbles have been made there for over a century. The museum is located in a former marble factory.

Historically, marbles have been used for pump valves, bottle stoppers, and in balloting. Voters used to cast a black marble for "no" and a white one for "yes." (This led to the exclusionary term, "blackballed.") Farther back in marble history, anthropologists report unearthing small, rounded stones from Stone Age digs on three continents. Moreover, marble games were played by ancient Greeks and Romans. Later, the tiny spheres are mentioned in fourteenth-century manuscripts and shown in a 1560 Flemish painting. In United States history, Presidents Washington, Jefferson, Lincoln, and Adams collected marbles. Garfield and Harrison even had their pictures sealed inside sulphide marbles. By 1899, there were twenty marble works in pre-tire Akron. According to the museum, the decline of marble playing, and collecting, began around 1950 as more school playgrounds were blacktopped so there was not as much dirt available in which kids could scratch marble rings. Also, TV was starting to consume children's spare time. Later, Nintendo and videos seemed to be the final nails in the coffin in which marble games were being buried.

Lately, however, playing and collecting marbles are enjoying a resurgence. There are five national organizations, many festivals and tournaments for all ages, and hundreds of serious collectors. The marble museum contains many of the early machines that made marbles, and retains an expert to evaluate old marbles visitors may have on hand. Also exhibited are the world's largest and smallest marbles. One is tinier than a pin's head while the other is seven inches in diameter. A few rare marbles are reportedly worth four thousand dollars.

If you're stuck fast on playing Nintendo, there's the National Video Game and Coin-Op Museum in St. Louis, which houses the very first video game, the 1971-vintage Computer Space, and its successor, Pong. Other early favorites like Donkey Kong and Pac-Man are displayed, along with low-tech pinball machines and artifacts.

Recently moved from New York City, the Dog Museum in St. Louis has two thousand pieces of dog-related sculpture, photos, paintings, and other canine art such as a special exhibit devoted to Snoopy drawings. One wing offers a roomful of videotapes on dog breeds and dog training.

However, because of too many canine "accidents" and too many fleas in the new facility, actual dogs are no longer welcome in the Dog Museum.

The same restriction is in effect at a showcase for restriction—the San Quentin Museum, located at California's oldest prison. The museum displays old restraining devices such as a nineteenth-century metal wrist cuff designed to tame rowdy inmates. Other artifacts include antique firearms, weapons handmade by inmates, old prison documents and photos, striped uniforms, *real* balls and chains, and leg irons. The curator points out that not everything that has happened over the years has been bad. For instance, during World War II, San Quentin prisoners donated blood, built lifeboats, made air raid sirens, and constructed a metal net to hang in the waters below the Golden Gate Bridge to stop Japanese subs.

San Quentin started as a prison ship in 1852. Later, inmates helped fill in part of San Francisco Bay and expand the prison site to 440 acres of bayside property. The museum contains a mock-up of the old gallows and the current gas chamber, which have taken the lives of 498 men and 4 women since 1873. (The prison was co-ed until 1933.) Other photo displays detail a mass escape made in 1862, when three hundred inmates dashed for freedom, and another in 1933, when four desperadoes broke out and made it to Corte Madera, fifteen miles away, before being cornered in a barn.

The Lock Museum of America, Inc., in Terryville, Connecticut, offers the history of locks in the United States and a few artifacts from lock-and-key history. The Lock Museum offers a four-thousand-year-old Egyptian-made pin-tumbler lock. Other displays include a cannonball safe, early time locks and door locks, padlocks, and more handcuffs.

The Barbed-Wire Museum in La Crosse, Kansas, promotes itself as the "Barbed Wire Capital of the World." The museum offers examples of about five hundred types of barbed wire, and much of the specialized equipment needed to make it. Barbed-wire collectors gather in La Crosse once a year in May and display, trade, or buy pices of the prickly wire. According to the museum, barbed wire is highly significant because it changed the landscape of the Great Plains by eliminating the free range; this started range wars and sparked debate about land-use policies in the West. Some enthusiasts credit the wire for the development of the tank in World War I, since hundreds of miles of barbed-wire fences helped create stalemate in the trenches. But the tank could roll right through barbed wire. Always displayed in eighteen-inch lengths, various sections of barbed wire bear not only sharp prongs but spurs, buckles, stars, leaves, and spirals.

Another barbed-wire collection, this one claiming to be the world's largest, is found in the Devil's Rope Museum in McLean, Texas. On hand are examples of concertina wire, the military's version of barbed wire—tightly coiled wire that is edged, not with barbs, but with rows of razor blades.

If anybody was tough-hided enough to sneak through concertina wire, the six-foot-six, 255-pound Sheriff Buford Pusser—who was shot eight times and knifed seven during his extraordinary career—would have been the guy to catch him. After Pusser's exploits as a crime-busting sheriff from 1964 to 1974 were portrayed on the silver screen in three *Walking Tall* movies, the state bought the sheriff's home in Adamsville, Tennessee, and turned it into the Buford Pusser Home & Museum. According to the museum, not quite everything in the movies actually happened. But during his lifetime, Pusser wrestled and defeated a grizzly bear, fought off six men at once (three were jailed, the others hospitalized), destroyed eighty-seven whiskey stills in 1965 alone, and suffered a shot-away jaw. Because of Pusser's war against moonshiners, gamblers, and organized crime, several assassination attempts were made on the lawman. In one, Pauline Pusser, Buford's wife, was shot and killed. Pusser himself was killed in a suspected attempt on his life when his Corvette went out of control and crashed in 1974. There are none of Pusser's huge oak bludgeons from the movies lying around the museum. Buford only used a club on the bad guys once, when he went to take back some stolen cash. On that occasion, he pulled a fence post from the ground and used it on the crooks. The remainder of Pusser's bludgeon swinging and bashing was pure Hollywood invention.

Other cops have their spots, too. The American Police Hall of Fame & Museum in Miami, Florida, is easily found because it has a full-sized police car attached several stories up on the building's facade. Inside, you'll find ten thousand police arti-facts—more vehicles, weapons, uniforms, badges (including "Wild Bill" Hickok's), an electric chair, Lee Harvey Oswald's autopsy photo, bricks from the garage where the Saint Valen-tine's Day massacre took place, a gas chamber, a guillotine, jail cells, and a mock crime scene where visitors are invited to "solve the murder." A four-hundred-ton slab of marble bears the en-graved names of some three thousand four hundred officers slain in the line of duty in the past thirty years.

The American Police Center & Museum in Chicago offers similar displays but features a lot more gangster memorabilia from the Prohibition era. One of John Dillinger's three death masks can be seen, as well as one of Bonnie Parker's favorite guns.

For some more serious enforcement, you may want to visit the Guided Missile Museum. Under construction at Point Mugu, California, the museum shows the history of guided missiles developed at Point Mugu after World War II with the help of German scientists who once worked under Hitler. In the collection are the "Loon" missile, the first missile fired at the base in 1946, the "Bat," the "Pelican" and "Sparrow I."

Many famous people, living and dead, have their own museums. For instance, at the Roy Rogers and Dale Evans Museum in Victorville, California, a stuffed Trigger, Rogers's horse, and Bullet, his dog, are on display among other personal paraphernalia like silver saddles, guitars, guns, cars, and letters from former United States presidents.

Lawrence Welk's boyhood home in Stasburg, North Dakota, became the Welk Museum when fans and supporters ponied up two hundred thousand dollars to recreate the home and family as it looked around 1890. Another Lawrence Welk Museum is in Escondido, California.

When Muppets creator Jim Henson got the idea for Kermit the Frog, he was inspired by the frogs along Deer Creek near his boyhood home in Leland, Mississippi. So the Muppets Museum was installed on the banks of Deer Creek. A marker commemorates the place as Kermit's birthplace.

Another favorite son, clown Emmett Kelly, has the Emmett Kelly Museum in Sedan, Kansas. It contains mementos from his many years with Ringling Brothers and Barnum & Bailey Circus and as leading bum with the Brooklyn Dodgers.

Billed as Nevada's third largest tourist attraction (after casino gambling and Hoover Dam), the Liberace Museum in Las Vegas, Nevada, contains enough glittering sequined outfits and rhinestoned vehicles to attract attention at the far edge of the Milky Way.

Robert L. Ripley, creator of the *Believe It Or Not!* cartoon series, also has his own museum. Located in Santa Rosa, California, the Ripley Memorial Museum is housed in The Church Built from One Tree. The building is so named because all the lumber used in its 1873 construction came from a single redwood tree—believe it or not. Contained in the building are: a life-sized wax figure of Ripley, a bust of the cartoonist sculpted by a blind man, the safari helmet Ripley wore on his travels, and other personal objects.

The Miss Ima Hogg Museum in Quitman, Texas, is named for the only daughter of Governor James Hogg. The museum contains Hogg family and Texas memorabilia.

The Fantastic Museum in Redmond, Oregon, started as owner Jim Schmit's personal collection of, well, *stuff*, three decades ago. The collection became a museum that now offers a mechanical clown band; a Laurel and Hardy stunt car; a full-sized mechanical elephant; Elizabeth Taylor's dressing room from *Cleopatra;* a trailer load of one million buttons; and two hours of some of the first known television commercials that play on a set (then known as a "commercial televisor") made in 1932. On the slightly morbid side, the museum offers a gauge that is the only remaining part of the *Hindenburg;* Olaf, a nine-foot mummified Viking (born about 1335, he was found in a peat bog in Norway in 1888); and the car in which the future president John F. Kennedy learned to drive. There are also remnants of a $1.5 million rocket-powered boat, *Discovery II,* which crashed on Lake Tahoe while trying to break the world's speed record on water, then over six hundred miles an hour.

Another collection of the bizarre can be found in the Museum of Jurassic Technology in Los Angeles. (Since the Jurassic geological era ended 140,000,000 years ago it handed down very little of its technology.) A "please touch" place, the museum's motto is: "The learner must be led always from familiar objects toward the unfamiliar . . . guided along, as it were, a chain of flowers into the mysteries of life." For instance, one exhibit, "Voice of the American Gray Fox," is arranged so the visitor looks through glasses aimed at a fox's head. He sees not the head of the fox, but a holographic video image of a large man sitting in a chair, barking like a fox. Other displays include the Deprong

Mori, a bat that allegedly can fly through walls; a collection of now-extinct nineteenth-century French moths; and an exhibit on "protective auditory mimicry" which tells about the supposed way beetles (the crawling insects) reproduce the sound of stones (as in rocks.) Yet another exhibit shows how the African stink ant can go bonkers, thanks to a local fungus, attach itself to a leaf high in a tree and wait in a drugged stupor for death.

The Mutter Museum at the College of Physicians in Philadelphia offers medical memorabilia dating from the 1840s to the present. On display are items like Chief Justice John Marshall's bladder stones, a piece of John Wilkes Booth's thorax, and a tumor taken from the jaw of President Grover Cleveland.

"Our exhibits are graphic and intensely real, but also a part of medical history," says Gretchen Worden, director of the Mutter Museum. "Artifacts on display here were once used to teach medicine. Preserved fetuses and other such 'teaching aids' were common in the nineteenth century in America and are still used elsewhere in the world."

On display is the skeleton of a man who stood seven foot six, the liver tissue of the famed Siamese twins Chang and Eng, and the world's most distended colon, dubbed the "megacolon." It is the size of a cow colon and once was contained within a five-foot-nine-inch man.

Another room contains Dr. Chevalier Jackson's collection of swallowed and inhaled foreign objects. Dr. Jackson, known as "the Father of Laryngology," retrieved from his patients' esophagi, lungs, and stomachs such things as jacks, safety pins, hat pins, tiny toys, several skate keys, bullets, nuts and bolts, alarm clock parts, false teeth, whistles, poker chips, radio knobs, and enough coins to start a bank. Among Dr. Jackson's many inventions was a long instrument that closes, and then removes from the stomach, safety pins that had been swallowed while open.

The National Museum of Health and Medicine in Washington, D.C., was founded during the Civil War as the Army

Medical Museum. It now combines the very modern with the very unusual. For instance, a few feet away from a modern AIDS display is a glass case containing the bones of the amputated right leg of Union general Daniel E. Sickles, who lost his limb at the Battle of Gettysburg. Somehow, the general had the presence of mind to collect and save the cannonball that struck him. He then sent the shattered leg and projectile to the museum in a coffin-shaped box. In later years, Sickles visited the museum on the anniversary of the battle to see his remains.

Other displays include items like mummified Siamese twins, a dissected human ear, a human foot, and a chewed-up pair of shorts found in the stomach of a shark. You can see some of Abraham Lincoln's bloodied clothing and seven small skull fragments removed after his autopsy. There is a section of President James Garfield's spinal column which bears the hole made by an assassin's bullet.

The Museum of Questionable Medical Devices in Minneapolis offers medical machines that never quite lived up to their lofty promises. A machine known as the Mycro-dynameter was supposed to measure skin resistance to electrical current, come up with a diagnosis, and then heal the patient. But when tested, it couldn't tell the difference between a live patient and a cadaver.

The Spectrochrome machine projected colored lights onto a patient's body to heal it of cancer and other maladies, but only worked if the patient sat in the nude, facing north during certain phases of the moon. Green light was claimed to cure arthritis while basic blues were said to take care of lung diseases. Followers of Spectrochrometry were organized into local congregations called planets. Each planet was headed by a Normalator who dispensed therapy and instructed his flock.

Loma Linda University in California has another collection of quack devices, assembled by the National Council Against Health Fraud, Inc. Many of the displays were seized by the Federal Food and Drug Administration from quacks. One such machine, the Ozone Generator, while worthless for treatment of forty-seven diseases for which it promised cures, lit up, buzzed, and produced ozone and oxides of nitrogen, gases which are irritating to the respiratory system and potentially toxic. Also known as the Vitozone, Purozone, Calozone (for sales in California), Nevazone (for Nevada sales), and Airozone (for Arizona), the units fetched $140 each and were most often bought by people with asthma or arthritis.

The Funk-Emanating Director was touted as a cure-all that could not only heal aches and pains but could also search out underground sources of oil. The Orgone Energy Accumulator, a five-foot-tall wooden box lined with zinc, was designed to attract a type of mysterious energy labeled orgone. Its primary advocate, Dr. Wilhelm Reich, a behavioral psychologist, believed orgone was the vital force which made humans healthy. By his reckoning, illness therefore was simply a lack of orgone. So, for good health, one simply—if expensively—recharged oneself with the precious stuff. You could go to a practitioner who had an Accumulator or you could buy your own for $275—a princely sum in the late 1930s. Dr. Reich, his own orgone level presumably depleted because of his dismal surroundings, died in prison in 1957.

The only known museum dedicated to feet (and some toes) belongs to Dr. Thomas Amberry, a Long Beach, California, podiatrist. Offering about nine thousand pieces of foot-related paraphernalia in six rooms and several murals of feet that decorate the walls around his parking lot, Dr. Amberry has in his office/museum one entire wall of vanity license plates carrying podiatric messages. A few plates read: "10 TOES," "BUNIONS," "CORNS," "FOOT HLR," "DRPOD," and so on. Also on display are foot-shaped lamps, a foot-shaped skateboard, the tiny boots of Gen. Tom Thumb, and the size twenty-six gunboats worn by George Bell, a seven-foot-eight-inch basketball player. The only foot-related acquisition Dr. Amberry bemoans lacking is an authenticated set of Bigfoot prints.

*   *   *

Other museums worth a visit:

- New Orleans Historic Voodoo Museum
- R. A. Kemp's Mack Truck Museum in Hillsboro, New Hampshire
- Surf Museum in Huntington Beach, California
- American Advertising Museum in Portland, Oregon
- Los Angeles Museum of Neon Art
- Fly Fishing Museum in Grants Pass, Oregon
- Buckhorn Hall of Horns at the Lone Star Brewery in San Antonio, Texas
- Museum of Cartoon Art in San Francisco
- Guitar Museum in Bristol, Tennessee
- Cowgirl Hall of Fame and Museum in Hereford, Texas
- Country Doctor Museum in Bailey, North Carolina
- Delta Blues Museum in Clarksdale, Mississippi
- Museum of Tobacco Art and History in Nashville, Tennessee
- Straw Museum in Dallas
- Strippers Hall of Fame and Museum at Exotic Ranch in Helendale, California.

5

MYTHICAL KINGDOMS AND
PRETENDING PRINCES

In the 1958 film *The Mouse That Roared*, the Duchy of Grand Fenwick claimed to be the world's smallest and least progressive nation. After suffering a terrible economic setback, the duchy decided the best way out was to declare war on the United States, knowing defeat was as certain as the reconstruction aid that would follow. When the peace treaty was signed, the duchy applied for five hundred thousand dollars to build a moon rocket. Instead, the United States responded with a full $1 million, while the Soviet Union bested the grant by giving Grand Fenwick the desired moon rocket.

The inhabitants of the duchy beat both Americans and Russians to the moon, claiming that celestial body as its sovereign territory.

In situations where life seems to have imitated art, a host of mavericks have created their own self-styled nations. Some of these little-known domains have proclaimed declarations of independence, adopted constitutions, designed coats-of-arms, minted coins, sent special envoys abroad, and issued stamps, passports, and visas. In some cases their freelance rulers have applied to larger nations for diplomatic recognition and the commercial benefits that follow. Usually, the request results in icy silence or a curt "no comment."

It's not exactly a new idea. In 1850, in Rough and Ready, a tiny town in northern California, a mining tax was laid on the citizens and enraged everybody. So the town broke away from California and declared itself the Great Republic of Rough and Ready. (The town's founder once served in the army under Zachary "Rough and Ready" Taylor.) But twelve weeks later, the republic wanted a big Fourth of July blowout more than independence, and rejoined California just before the Fourth. The only reminder of the great republic is a yearly two-month celebration in Rough and Ready—Secession Days.

Some founders of would-be nations have laid claim to bits and snatches of the earth's surface that could be generously described as remote. Some of these places don't even have any territory because they're under water most of the time.

For instance, somewhere in the island-dotted South China Sea is the Republic of Morac-Songhrati-Meads. Formerly known as the Kingdom of Humanity, that nation was founded by American businessman Morton F. Meads, who declared himself king. Meads contends his claim is legitimate because he is descended from a sea captain, George Meads, who discovered the islands in the 1870s while sailing under the British flag. At the time, the empire-rich British had no use for the tiny islands, many of which were under water at high tide, so Meads claimed them for himself and his family.

Meads established a constitutional monarchy about thirty years ago, located his capital on a rocky outcropping dubbed Meads Island, and selected Ludwig van Beethoven's Fifth Symphony as the national anthem.

Morac-Songhrati-Meads applied to the United States, Switzerland, the International Postage Union, the Philippines, and anybody else with a mailbox for official recognition. But its efforts mostly resulted in a search by Philippine Air Force jets for the new republic to see if it really existed and, if so, if anything illegal was going on out there. All this happened in the late 1950s when the Philippines were very concerned about communists.

"Illegal activities" then included making unflattering remarks about the government in print or in speech, holding public meetings about anything and, especially, carving out a new nation so close to the Philippines.

But war, or even the usual brand of right-wing repression, never broke out because the Air Force pilots couldn't find the place.

In 1985, an unsuccessful lawsuit was filed in the Morac-Songhrati-Meads Court of Special Cases, Pennsylvania VI Island, against an array of United States officials, government agencies, and companies. The lawsuit sought at least $25 billion in damages for infringement, unfair competition, harassment, and sabotage. At the heart of the matter was a claim on other islands and, coincidentally enough, oil rights in the strategically located Spratly chain of islands, which are better described as a series of reefs. The Spratly Islands lie 500 miles off the coast of Vietnam. While the islands and outcroppings are spread across an area measuring 500 miles by about 560 miles, the total area of the above-water islands is less than two square miles. During World War II, Japan kept a submarine base there but then relinquished all claims after the conflict. China, Taiwan, South Vietnam, Malaysia, and the Philippines made claims on some or all of the islands.

Today, Malaysia, China, and Vietnam are rattling rockets about each other's outposts in the Spratlys, while Morac-Songhrati-Meads keeps its usual low profile.

Another pipsqueak nation in the South Seas, the Republic of Minerva, "The Land of the Rising Atoll," is dry for only several hours a day. Essentially, Minerva is a scattering of rocks exposed by low tides. Nonetheless, a group of American businessmen, asserting that the area was unclaimed, declared sovereignty in 1972 and set out to build a nation with no welfare, foreign aid, income tax, or armed forces. The new nation was to serve as a commerce and banking center. Its official flag was a torch of freedom on a background field of blue. A California electrical engineer became provisional president of Minerva and oversaw the construction of small platforms on the rocks, which are within the North and South Minerva reefs about four hundred miles south of Fiji. Requests for recognition were sent to a hundred established nations, with one positive reply—Occussi Ambeno, a tiny island in the Timor Sea was sympathetic and granted recognition because it had also suffered the indignity of nonrecognition so many times. But Minerva's closest established neighbor, the Kingdom of Tonga, not only refused recognition, but quickly dispatched a crew of ninety convicts to build larger platforms over the Minervan platforms, haul down the upstart's flag and, as a public service, leave beacons and survival kits on each platform. The mission wasn't entirely without incident, however. The convicts broke into a brawl and several were hospitalized. Later, Tonga announced sovereignty over the Minervan reefs. Undaunted, the founding fathers of Minerva opened negotiations with Tonga and the Minervan plans seemed to be going forward. The president said they had applications for citizenship from two thousand-odd people. "That's many more than we have room for," he said.

In 1985, King and Absolute Ruler Mitchara Heatara signed a declaration of independence that established the Maori Kingdom of Tetiti Island in the South Pacific. He wanted to give the Maori people, "a race that is speeding to oblivion," a place to "call their own, their rightful place in the sun." His special envoy offered the United States a long-term lease on one island, located about five hundred miles from the New Zealand coast. It seemed like a good deal but when the United States geographer looked closely at the islands of the Tetiti kingdom, he found that a dozen or so—Raoul, Bounty, Campbell, Aukland, and others—already belong to other nations.

*   *   *

Another "country," Atland, was completely covered by
water. A businessman in Maryland once learned the water south
of Newfoundland had a depth of only thirty-five feet and that
it would be possible to build an offshore airport by building up
the ocean floor. So he declared Atland a kingdom and marked it
with a radar-reflecting buoy. For a while, there was a listing for
Atland in the Washington, D.C., *Yellow Pages* under "Embassies."
Atland also applied to the United Nations and other countries
for recognition, but got nowhere.

In 1948, a hopelessly addicted fisherman, Russell Arundel,
in union with his fishing buddies, founded the Principality of
Outer Baldonia. The new country consisted of four small is-
lands—Little Bald Island, Half Bald Island, Little Half Bald
Island, and Outer Bald Tusket—near the coast of Nova Scotia.
Arundel's official title was Prince of Princes.

Eventually, Arundel bought the islands, minted coins (the
basic unit of which was the tunar), and printed stationery that
bore an official Outer Baldonia seal. Arundel brought forth a
new nation founded on the principles of drinking, swearing,
gambling, and the freedoms to go unshaven and to lie about the
size of fish. He established the value of his nation's currency each
day at the cocktail hour and once declared war on the Soviet
Union, although hostilities never broke out. For a while there
was a tiny Washington, D.C., office that served as the Outer
Baldonia Embassy to the United States. A small "castle" was
built on the main island from which the principality could be
ruled. Later, the Baldonia islands were donated for use as a bird
sanctuary.

In 1967, Roy and Joan Bates, a couple in Southend-on-Sea,
Essex, England, took over an abandoned World War II radar and
gun platform in the North Sea about six miles from the British
coast. The new steel and concrete nation was christened the
"Principality of Sealand," with Roy serving as Prince, Joan as

Princess, and son Michael filling various other positions as heads of state. The purpose of Sealand was to serve as a free port and free-trade area. For the last twenty-five years, plans have been in the offing to issue stamps, currency, passports, and tax advantages. Once known as Roughs Tower, Sealand has no income or inheritance taxes, but intends to raise revenues through tax stamps, offshore registration of companies, ships and yachts, hotels, a casino, an international lottery, and other schemes.

The international business community has been fascinated with Sealand, but nothing much has materialized so far. At one time or another, plans were made to expand the three-acre platform by four thousand acres for a specially designed golf course and a spacious convention center. The plans didn't say if the course greens would be natural, imported turf or just concrete painted green.

Roy Bates recently told an English newspaper: "Once or twice a month, I'm approached by businessmen with ideas. There's always a good lunch, some very decent wine, and then I tend not to hear from them again."

Bates, once the British army's youngest major, is probably the right person to own a nation so close to England. During the Falklands war, Bates was approached by agents from Argentina who wanted to buy Sealand so their country could have their own "Malvinas" right on Britain's doorstep. Of course, the Major refused their offer and their wine and sent the blackguards packing.

Prince Roy, Princess Joan, and their international lawyers contend that Britain, by abandoning the tower after World War II, had performed a dereliction of sovereignty. Britain recently extended its territorial waters to a twelve-mile limit and maintains that Sealand is now back under jurisdiction of the crown. The Bateses use their Sealand passports when traveling; however, their stamps won't take a letter very far.

Currently, all power seems to rest with Prince Roy. However, as soon as enough people show up he intends to create a

senate. The only subjects residing on Sealand now are usually
three or four security guards.

The mythological nation of Atlantis was a continent in the
Atlantic that sank beneath the waves sometime before the birth
of Christ. But the story of Atlantis did not end in prehistory.

In 1933, Captain J. L. Mott, a fifty-three-year-old sea captain from Denmark, discovered he was related to the Viking
explorer, Leif Ericson. That was especially significant to Mott
because, in the year A.D. 930, Ericson wrote that he had discovered in the Caribbean the fourteen remaining islands of Atlantis that had not sunk. So, on March 5, 1934, Captain Mott
wrote to the International Postage Union, explaining that he had
laid claim to the islands, which were the remnants of the lost
continent. According to Mott, the islands "were to the east and
west of the Isthmus of Panama and would be used for scientific
experiments." Later, Mott told the U.S. State Department the
islands had not been claimed by anyone, that Atlantis should be
the natural home for all explorers, and that he was going to hold
an exposition of art, inventions, and other products there.

In 1936, Mott told the Long Island Daily Advocate that
historians and scientists were among many settlers. They had
found evidence that their nation was once part of the famed lost
continent. Captain Mott applied several times for membership
in the International Postal Union so that other nations would
honor his triangular Atlantis stamps. When New York City reporters asked to see his fleet, Mott could only show them one
ship, a leaking four-masted schooner docked at Staten Island. He
also claimed to have twenty-five thousand backers, but they
turned out to be a few people with more curiosity than money.
Moreover, Mott's letters home to Denmark kept coming back
because he mailed them from New York with Atlantis stamps.
Mott's one-page constitution provided for no taxes, declared the
nation would never, ever use force against anybody, and conceded
that some people could mistake Atlantis for sandbars. Soon, Mott

was trying to sell Atlantis coins and claimed that Ecuador had recognized his nation.

On April 17, 1936, Mott livened things up at an otherwise sleepy border post when he tried to use his Atlantis passport to enter the United States at El Paso. But the guards weren't that sleepy and didn't buy it for a moment, and Mott finally used his Danish passport. The following day, an El Paso newspaper ran the story under the headline: "Atlantis Citizen Enters El Paso After Giving Inspectors a Lesson in Geography."

That lesson included the latest developments in the Principality of Atlantis. An island, Odino, had been named as the nation's capital; the islands Flamingo and Thoro had been added; Esperanto was the official language; and the unit of currency was the "skaloj," one hundred of which made a "dalo." One dalo was then said to be worth fifty United States cents. Atlantis stamps bore the likeness of the then seventy-nine-year-old Marie, wife of Denmark's Prince Regent Christian I. Nonetheless, Mott's letters home were still being returned, marked "postage due." According to Mott, those twenty-five thousand backers had now become citizens, all of whom were said to be busily growing tropical fruit for shipment to Norway, Denmark, and Germany. And there had been a name change. The nation was now known as "Empire of Atlantis and Lemuria."

In 1947, Gertude Anna Meeker of Hollywood, California, wrote President Truman, asking where she could find the "Atlantis-Lemuria Government." Truman didn't have much advice but Gertrude apparently found somebody who knew, because seven years later, in 1954, Meeker reappeared as an ardent spokesperson for Atlantis and Lemuria. An elaborate letterhead with an official seal of state noted that the name of the nation was Imperi Atlantis Kaj Lemuria. ("Kaj" is Esperanto for "and.") Meeker lived at the nation's information bureau in Laguna Beach, California. She also described herself as a "Realestate (sic) Broker of Calif. and a Mining Executive of the U.S.A. and anywhere for that matter." Meeker spent much of the 1950s mulling over renouncing her American citizenship in order to become Queen of the Pacific Empire of Atlantis and Lemuria. But her letters bearing Atlantis stamps kept coming back, too, so she didn't get much done.

By 1958, the island empire and "all rights, titles, and properties of the Atlantic and Pacific Empire of Atlantis and Lemuria, a nonunion and noncommunist government," had passed on to Ms. Meeker, who now listed herself as Governor General.

We know so much about Atlantis and other maverick nations because the Office of the Geographer at the U.S. Department of State in Washington, D.C., is charged with checking on such places. When members of the state department receive letters from people who claim to be the head of a new nation, it's the task of the Office of the Geographer to see if the place really exists and is recognized by other nations. So a file officially known as "Ephemeral States," but sometimes privately referred to as the "Mythical Kingdoms, Kooky Kings, and Pretending Princes" is kept. The forty-year-old file contains letters of credentials, declarations, affidavits, and maps from people claiming to have started their own countries. Many of the memos in the file are from United States government officials wanting to know if there is such a place as Nation X or Principality Y.

America's official geographers have looked at the claims several times and found that all the islands in the area claimed to be Atlantis are already owned by sovereign states. And that includes sandbars.

Says Bill Wood, director of the Office of the Geographer: "To be a state, the place must have a definite territory and the government must have control over the population within its territory. If the U.N. recognizes it, you can be pretty sure it's a real nation."

Other wanna-be nations included in Wood's ephemeral file include: Luconia, the Principality of Thomond, Aphrodite, the Kingdom of Lundy, the Nation of Aryan-Pacific, the People's Democratic Republique of Quay, and the Principality of Castellania, created by a group of disenchanted Austrians in 1974. Its location, somewhere in the South Pacific, was kept secret, although one of its leaders admitted, "Castellania is more a state of mind." The King of the Mosquito Shore and Nation, on the east coast of Central America, also wrote to the United States looking for an official relationship. Another writer claimed he had found places named the Republic of the Isle of Dogs and the Kingdom of Yap.

But of all the letters, memos, and other notes, the fifty-year-old saga of Atlantis is the longest. And it didn't go away quickly.

In 1964, Leicester Hemingway, author of the book, *My Brother, Ernest Hemingway*, founded tiny New Atlantis on an eight-foot by thirty-foot platform of bamboo logs floating in the sea about seven miles away from Jamaica. New Atlantis gained a type of official recognition when Leicester printed a batch of his country's first-issue stsamps and sent them (inside an envelope, alas) to then-United States President Lyndon B. Johnson. The U.S. State Department responded, thanking him in a letter addressed to "Leicester Hemingway, Acting President, Republic of New Atlantis." It was the first time in history the stamps of an upstart nation had actually traveled somewhere.

Later, Hemingway told the *New York Times:* "I can stand on the platform, walk around on it, and salute the flag, all of which I do periodically. There are no taxes here, because taxes are for people not smart enough to start their own countries."

Hemingway also wanted lebensraum for New Atlantis so that he and the seven other citizens could all have lunch there at once. But the country disappeared when scavenging fishermen picked apart the national planks for scrap. Towering seas claimed the remainder of New Atlantis, which had been moored to the shallow sea bottom with an anchor and an old Ford engine block. In January 1973, Hemingway emerged again as president of another artificial island, this time, the Republic of Tierra del Mar, located on the Great Bahama Bank about thirty miles east of

Bimini. Again, the purpose of the new republic was for marine research and perhaps to dodge a tax or two. But nothing much happened, and since then all of modern-day Atlantis—along with its founding fathers and mothers—seems to have sunk back under the waves.

In October, 1969, the government of Western Australia issued to farmer Leonard George Casely a wheat allotment through a Wheat Quota Board that he found impossibly low. After a flurry of letters protesting to Australia's prime minister, the governor of Western Australia, and others, Casely decided there was nothing else he could do but turn his 18,500 acre farm into a separate nation. So on March 21, 1970, Casely sent notice of an act of secession to all the government officials who had received his previous letters about the low wheat quota. Henceforth, Casely would be known as His Royal Highness, Prince Leonard. Moreover, his farm was now the Hutt River Province Principality, a sovereign state, and would grant allegiance only to Queen Elizabeth II, if she would have it. Prince Leonard then applied for membership in the United Nations and in the Commonwealth of British Nations.

In the Australian government, nothing much was done about the secession. The prime minister thought the matter rightly belonged to the state of Western Australia. The governor of the state thought the Hutt River Province secession was a matter for constitutional scholars to solve. Judges wanted a ruling in Parliament or a precedent case. Finally, Casely called and asked a government official if he, Casely, might find the Australian army on his rebellious doorstep some morning. The official admitted, "We're not doing anything about the secession."

Somewhat inspired, Casely set up a government, designed a flag, picked an official seal and motto, and went about the business of running his principality. It is organized something like the government of Liechtenstein, with a constitution and a single-house parliament to which members are elected every five years.

The first real conflict with the government of Australia was not about secession but about mail. People all over the world had read about the Hutt River Province and were sending letters to Casely. But the Australian post office declared that, officially, there was no such place as the Hutt River Principality and no such person as Prince Leonard. Moreover, the International Postal Union never answered Casely's request for membership, so Hutt stamps were declared "stickers" and not valid for moving mail. (However, if you mailed a letter to anybody inside the twenty-nine-square-mile Hutt River Principality, you would have to use an official Hutt stamp.) Just like Captain Mott in New York City so many years before, correspondents sending letters outside the principality had their mail returned if they did not use a proper Aussie stamp.

After three months without mail, Casely started one of his whirlwind letter-writing campaigns. Soon a compromise was reached. The Australian post office collected mail addressed to His Royal Highness or to Hutt at the nearby Northampton post office, where Casely rented a post office box. Then, postal workers delivered it to the principality. Hutt citizens could affix their own stamps to outgoing mail as long as they also paid one of the Australian postmasters for the correct postage.

There must be a lot of letter writing going on inside the principality. Some fifty-one different stamps of various denominations have been issued in thirteen editions. Hutt stamps depict local flowers and fauna, religious figures, scenes in the principality, and the sun-weathered visage of His Royal Highness Leonard himself. Coinage includes a Silver Jubilee dollar, dedicated to England's Queen Elizabeth II, and a five-dollar coin commemorating Desert Storm.

Court cases, however, aren't quite as easily solved. Usually, when in court, Casely points out there is a two-year statute of limitations on both the state of Western Australia and the national government of Australia about acting on the 1970 secession. Nothing had been done; therefore, any time Casely or any other Hutt citizen was hauled into court, they would be there under duress. And using duress is illegal. Case dismissed. Usually.

One case occurred when Prince Arthur Wayne, one of Casely's sons, was prosecuted by Australia for not properly signing up for the draft. The prince was hauled into court. Casely found and dusted off an old law saying young men in Australia from other nations could request to be deported to their own country when checking in at boot camp. Prince Arthur Wayne arrived at basic training camp but before he had time to fill out the papers requesting deportation, the Commonwealth of Australia acted on its own and shipped him back to the Hutt River Province. It was an age-related draft.

When it comes to the matter of taxes, Casely says he finds himself "popping in and out of court" every time a new government is elected. Casely says he pays no taxes to the government of Australia and has escaped doing so by lengthy, complicated negotiations with the tax authorities and by appearing in court and using fine points of law. His worst defeat in court was when he was fined four dollars and spent two nights in jail because he would not pay the fine.

On December 2, 1977, Casely formally declared war on Australia but called it off two days later, saying his government would now accept diplomatic relations with Australia. Casely then pointed out sections of international law to which Australia was a signatory, which stated that if an upstart nation—as is the Hutt River Province—is undefeated in warfare, then sovereignty is automatic when peace breaks out.

But, alas, while there are over ten thousand people throughout the world carrying Hutt River Province passports, and thirty permanent Hutt residents, Australia still does not recognize Casely's former farm. His Royal Highness says the Vatican has appointed a diplomatic delegate to his domain although he can't talk the Holy Father into accepting Hutt postage stamps. Casely says he has diplomatic appointees in about twenty-seven *real* nations around the world.

Casely built a small motel to accommodate visitors to his principality, and tries to insure a good time for all by sponsoring several sporting events every year. The principality usually has an entry in the Singapore Airlines London-Sydney Car Rally.

Casely quit growing wheat for twelve years, and eventually had the pleasure of seeing disbanded the Wheat Quota Board that started it all.

On his way to the New World, Christopher Columbus sailed by a deserted, rocky island he named Redonda. The island sat uninhabited and unclaimed in the Caribbean until 1865, when Matthew Dowdy Shiell, an Irish trader, happened to sail by. Shiell already had nine daughters, and was so overjoyed when a son was born that he declared the newborn King of Redonda when he sailed by the island. A decade and a half later, a local priest actually crowned young Shiel (he was to drop the final "l") in a ceremony on the island's highest peak. This was very important to the senior Shiell, who believed he was descended from Irish kings but had never received his proper due. Not long afterward, Shiel—dubbed Filipe I—was sent to college in England. Eventually, M. P. Shiel became a successful writer and still has a following today. (The movie *The World, the Flesh and the Devil*, with Harry Belafonte, was based on Shiel's book *The Purple Cloud*.) But meanwhile, back on Redonda, somebody discovered that guano—solidified bird droppings—sold well. So Britain formally annexed Redonda, despite years of protest by the senior Shiell. When Shiel died, his literary executor, John Gawsworth, started calling himself Juan I of Redonda and inherited everything, including the actual crown of Redonda which somehow got lost. Thereafter, for the price of a pint in a pub, a person could become a Duke of Redonda. So writers like Dylan Thomas, Lawrence Durrell, Henry Miller, Rebecca West, and others were awarded dukedoms, knighthoods, the "Star of Redonda," and other such honors. Gawsworth once tried to sell the crown of Redonda for one thousand pounds, but the island's nobles stopped him after he cashed a fifty-pound down payment from the crown prince of Sweden.

Over the years, writers of some note traded barbed comments with the government of England about who really owned Redonda. In the late 1940s, a bureaucrat suggested stationing somebody on the island to stop "the fad of nibbling at bits of the empire."

Today, the King of Redonda, Juan II, is publisher and novelist Jon Wynne-Tyson of Sussex, England. He is the first monarch to set foot on Redonda since Filipe I was crowned there. His trip was sponsored by an American who is a great fan of Shiel's writings. When the party arrived, they found the mining operation had long disappeared and there seemed to be nobody there. So the flag of Redonda was planted, a proclamation read, and toasts raised. Much to everybody's surprise, Juan II's entourage found a fully uniformed postmaster selling stamps on the island in a rickety post office. The only permanent inhabitants were goats and other wild creatures.

When Antigua claimed independence from Britain, she took Redonda with her. The postmaster, who doesn't really have anything to post, mans his office twice a week just so Antigua will have an official presence of some type on Redonda, thereby keeping it out of the hands of distant pretenders, all of whom seem to live in England. But at least the stamps on Redonda will get a letter sent home.

Although the Wynne-Tysons never use their titles in England, they did spend a winter as royalty in residence on Redonda while Jon wrote a book, *So Say Banana Bird*. The plot may sound somewhat familiar to you by now; it's about an Englishman who is king of a distant island.

*   *   *

If you want to skip all the trouble of creating and ruling your own nation, you can always have it just LOOK as though you're from an out-of-the-way nation by having a special passport made. Donna Walker of International Documents Service in Houston, Texas, designs and sells "camouflage" passports for travelers who fear war or hijackers and don't want to reveal their true nationalities.

"There are people traveling the world with passports stating they are citizens of Danzig, Ceylon, and the Island Republic of San Cristobal," Walker says. "Actually, Danzig was consumed in World War II, Ceylon became Sri Lanka and there's no such place as the Island Republic of San Cristobal. Right now, I'm working on a passport from an English-speaking country known as Klactu-Lactuburda. 'Klactu-Lactuburda' was a code word in the movie *The Day the Earth Stood Still*."

During the Gulf War, several Americans calmly walked across the Iraq-Jordan border, out of certain captivity and possible death, by flashing classy-looking passports from nations that do not exist.

Since virtually all the territory on earth is already taken, David Owen, a writer for *The Atlantic Monthly*, claimed the sun in the name of his publication. He then wrote to request official recognition from the U.S State Department, requesting: "The sun should now be referred to as the Solar Atlantic Empire, and I, henceforth, will be known as Lord High Suzerain of Outer Space."

The State Department says Owen's claim will be considered when he sends in his "pertinent state documents (a constitution, declarations, etc.), map of state, and evidence of recognition of his sovereign status by the majority of recognized states of Earth." So Owen is now looking for citizens to people his empire and for national leaders interested in setting up diplomatic relations with his sunny regime. Owen insists the Solar Atlantic Empire will never, ever declare war.

*   *   *

For a few days, a mythical nation, Ahad El Budy, existed in the halls and offices of Congress and in the minds of some of our elected representatives. During one of the Arab-inspired oil shortages, someone at the tabloid newspaper the *National Enquirer* thought inquiring minds would like to know how much influence Arabs from oil-rich nations could command in the offices of our lawmakers in Washington, D.C., if they, the Arabs, just walked in cold off the streets and started snapping their fingers. So, four swarthy *Enquirer* reporters donned white flowing robes and head-dresses, rented the longest stretch limo they could find, appointed one of their number "translator," and then—without appointments, guides, introductions, credentials, or bonafides—breezed into the Washington offices of representatives and senators. The "Sheik of Ahad El Budy" mouthed Arabic-sounding gibberish which was then put into English by an especially cowed bowing-and-scraping flunky who acted as the official "translator."

The scam worked like a charm for most of the day as the "sheik" and his followers breezed in and out of the offices of well-known members of Congress, seeking goodwill and favor for the sheikdom. In most cases, the "Arabs" were immediately ushered into inner sanctums, past high-level visitors who were waiting with appointments made weeks in advance. In a few cases, legislators left meetings to meet the "sheik" and receive his greetings.

Then, high on confidence and mouthing commands in Arabic-gibberish faster than ever, the "sheik" and his hangers-on breezed into the office of U.S. Senator James Abourezk, a South Dakota Democrat of Lebanese extraction. Flushed with success and now thinking about asking to borrow an aircraft carrier group or maybe the Seventh Pacific Fleet, the group went into their act, the humble "translator" bowing and scraping more than ever.

The reporters could barely conceal their shock and confusion when Senator Abourezk ignored the translator and spoke to the "sheik" directly in fluent Arabic. Abourezk was then the only elected official in Congress who spoke that language.

Stammered the "translator": "Ah so. Will forgive please. His majesty speaks an unusual dialect."

Recalled former Senator Abourezk about meeting the "ruler" of Ahad El Budy: "When I got nothing but mumbling from the 'sheik,' my first thought was my Arabic was getting rusty. I had never heard of the kingdom of Ahad El Budy, so the visitors explained it was an island in the Persian Gulf. I had the 'sheik' come into my office immediately because I thought he was the ruler of a nation. But then I noticed the 'sheik' was very light-skinned. And nobody from the Gulf is that light. Also, he carried his hands inside the sleeves of his costume, like a Chinese mandarin. As soon as they left, I told my secretary to check on them with the State Department. And the answer came back there was no such nation. I then called Jack Anderson who knew one of the reporters involved. Anderson wrote a column that week exposing the caper, so I figured that would ruin the story. But the *Enquirer* printed it anyhow."

As for the Sheik of Ahad El Budy and his entourage, they ran from the building as fast as their feet would carry them and came very close to being arrested. Several were chased by federal police as far as downtown Washington, where the reporters rejoined the Western world by ducking into a men's rest room to ditch their headdresses and flowing robes and then catching a subway.

6
ESOTERIC EMPLOYMENT

When Elihu Root, United States lawyer, statesman, and a 1912 Nobel Peace Prize winner, was in his late eighties, he hired a young man to read for him. One day, Root asked the reader what kind of occupation he intended to hold. Sol M. Linowitz, the reader, said he wasn't sure: perhaps he would be a rabbi or perhaps a lawyer.

Replied Root immediately: "Be a lawyer. A lawyer needs twice as much religion as a rabbi."

Chances are that Mr. Root would be a little less quick with advice were he alive today. How, for instance, would he have reacted to a choice between such jobs as mother repairer, slime plant operator, pickle pump operator, knock-up assembler, and whizzer?

A mother repairer is not a person who works on broken-down women who have children. Rather, it's a person who works with the master from which vinyl stereo records are pressed. While a mother tester is a full-time job every teenager has held at one time or another, it is also the person who inspects metal phonograph record "mothers" for defects.

A slime plant operator actually touches nothing disgusting; his task is to work with equipment that recovers precious metals from by-products used in refineries and smelting plants. And a pickle pump operator works not in a cucumber patch but in a slaughterhouse, injecting beef with a briny solution to help cure the meat. The knock-up assembler has nothing to do with putting anybody in a family way. The job involves fitting together pre-cut pieces of wood. A whizzer need not work faster than anybody else; his or her task is to operate machines that finish felt hats.

Requiring no machinery at all except a hand-held bell, Redmond O'Colonies claims to be the only town crier west of the Mississippi River. The official town crier of Martinez, California, O'Colonies says he is one of six or seven town criers in the United States and 350 worldwide. He represented the United States in the 1991 World Town Crying Championships, held in England.

"A town crier's job is to serve as an ambassador of goodwill to his community and to add a dash of color and theater," O'Colonies says. "He also encourages tourists to get out of their cars and take the air in his community."

O'Colonies's duties include opening town and community events with a specially written, two-minute cry that always begins with "Oyez, oyez," an ancient French word that means "gather and listen."

" 'Hear Ye! Hear Ye!' is strictly a Hollywood invention," says O'Colonies, who additionally offers Bell-'O-Grams for private functions. His working clothes include a tricorne hat, white tights, powdered white wig, breeches, and vest, as would be worn by a gentleman in Europe around 1750. A professional association, Brothers and Sisters of the Bell, represents the world's town criers.

Robert E. Harris, a full-time Baptist pastor in Asheville, North Carolina, is considered the last circuit-riding preacher. Harris rides a sorrel horse, Sundance, and wears full Western regalia with a black frock coat, string tie, and a ten-gallon Stetson hat. Harris rides his "circuit" most weekdays around Interstate 40 west of Asheville and hands out to resting motorists brochures with the history of circuit-riding preachers and a few religious messages.

Also working in another industry seemingly alone in its class is Marge Carlson, owner of the California School for Artistry in Whistling, the only professional whistling school in the nation. One of just a few full-time, professional whistlers in the United States, Carlson not only teaches the art of just putting your lips together, puckering up, and blowing, she performs regularly at conventions, and has produced three whistling cassettes. She gives forty to fifty concerts a year and specializes in gospel music.

"Whistling is an athletic activity," Carlson says. "It requires abdominal strength and strong lungs." Her repertoire includes show tunes, popular songs, melodies, and bird song imitations. Whistling, according to Mrs. Carlson, crosses all language barriers and is used in many cultures to communicate as well as to entertain.

"For instance, the stock report is whistled in the Canary Islands every day at noon," she says. "Moreover, among certain Indian tribes in Mexico, only men are allowed to whistle messages."

The Whistling Midgets of Davenport, Washington, do their act only part-tme, but if you're hungry for whistling, it's better than nothing. Three average-height men developed a skit wherein each wears a huge top hat, pulled down to conceal his shoulders and arms. They paint faces on their bare chests and abdomens, with their belly buttons forming the center of their "mouths." False arms hang from their hips. Recorded whistling is played and the men gyrate their stomachs like whistling faces.

Cheryl Lander also uses her lungs professionally, but not for something as gentle as whistling. A professional screamer, you've heard Cheryl scream in horror movies, in commercials, and in other productions. For instance, the blood-chilling scream that accompanies Alfred Hitchcock's television segments is her work. "A good scream starts with the diaphragm and is a full-body experience," Cheryl says. "Screaming is just a natural talent that I've passed on to my fourteen-year-old daughter, who is just starting out in screaming."

Joe and Suzanne Davis of Clear Lake, Texas, were pretty good at locating things, so they started their own firm, Finders Co., in 1965. As "findologists," the Davises have tracked down such things as a whiskey boat that sank in 1889, the keys to Adolph Hitler's mountaintop retreat, and even a long-retired bank robber. A client once converted an old bank into a restaurant and thought of having the infamous bank robber Willie Sutton there for the grand opening. The Davises found Sutton, living unobtrusively in a very average neighborhood. The sunken whiskey boat was tougher. After a lot of research, the Davises found the river had changed its course after the boat was lost, and it was buried in what had become a farmer's cornfield. (The client wanted to hand out small samples of the lost, century-old whiskey to advertise a new brand.) One order that completely stumped the Davises was a request for an original death cart used to haul bodies away during the Black Plague in Europe in the fourteenth century. The carts probably had all been burned, the Davises figure.

Another type of locating specialist works as a celebrity cast-offs specialist. Edi Boxstein turned celebrity scavenging into a full-time business known as Celebrity Knick-Knacks. Charities send Boxstein a laundry list of items and then pay her an hourly fee to go hunting. She obtains the item, often autographed, from the celebrity and turns it over to the charity which, in turn, auctions the knickknacks.

"I still have trouble convincing George Burns his cigar butts are valuable," Mrs. Boxstein says. "But I've seen them go for as much as eighty-five dollars each. He's always pleased to learn that his old cigar ends, coffee cups, and the like have raised money for schools, child abuse prevention programs, and other worthy causes."

Boxstein figures about a hundred thousand dollars have been

raised for charities. Moreoever, about twenty-five celebrities regularly donate cast-offs to Boxstein.

Elvira Ballard of Salmon, Idaho, is a masking tape artist. For the last twenty years, she has sculptured figures, mostly of Indians, from masking tape. She works with masking tape because it reminds her of buckskin. She makes two masking tape sculptures a week, and sells them for $28 to $40 each to supplement her Social Security stipend.

Another business that requires a fine eye and steady hand is miniature book maker. Pat Baldwin, of Bisbee, Arizona, makes and sells tiny books no taller than three inches. Her first such book, *The Monarch*, easily fits in the palm of the hand and contains about five thousand butterfly wings on pages that pull out of the tiny tome like an accordion. Her books sell for $60 to $125 each. One boxed miniature trilogy sold for $220. Her newest publication, a book of poetry, isn't off her lilliputian press yet.

The workaday task for Ashleigh Brilliant, the world's only full-time professional epigrammatist, is to reduce complex thoughts into easily digestible, often unforgettable nuggets. He calls these illustrated pearls "Pot Shots," which appear on T-shirts, shopping bags, coffee mugs, paperweights, and in fourteen of the nation's larger newspapers. Moreover, he's filled seven books with his drawings and epigrams. An example is, "We're in this together but there's always room for one less."© One man had a Brilliant epigram carved on his tombstone, "Before I knew the best part of my life had come, it had gone."©

Not only writers live by their senses. Some jobs require a sharp sense of taste. Take, for instance, ice cream taster John Harrison at Dreyer's Grand Ice Cream. East of the Rockies, the ice cream is known as "Edy's Grand." Harrison, whose tongue is insured for a cool $1 million, grew up in the ice cream industry. His great-grandfather, father, and uncle were all ice cream makers. Harrison's job is tasting all of Dreyer's sixty flavors, three times a day. Just by tasting a quarter of a spoonful, Harrison can tell if the ice cream is correct in cream, sugar, and flavoring. The samples are pulled from factories in Los Angeles, Denver, and Fort Wayne, Indiana. Plus, there are six styles of ice cream: light, low-fat frozen yogurt, cholesterol-free, sugar-free, nonfat frozen yogurt, and premium. To protect his sensitive tongue, Harrison shuns tobacco, alcohol, and spicy foods like curry-laden dishes or anything containing cayenne or Szechuan seasonings. "I try not to cuss, either," says Harrison, whose morning drink is never coffee but tepid tea—so he won't scald or dull his tongue. Moreover, he can't wear cologne because smelling is a large part of tasting. Harrison also supervises two other ice cream tasters at other plants. Harrison's tongue is sensitive enough to tell the difference between various brands of ice cream, and the percentage of butterfat each contains. He uses a gold-plated spoon because he can taste the residues on wood or plastic spoons.

Another educated palate is found in the mouth of chemist Don Williams, who is employed at Frito-Lay in Texas, where he tastes at least a pound of chips a day. While Williams has a Ph.D. in chemistry, his taste buds do a lot of his work for him. When he tastes chips with onions, he can tell if the onions came from Mexico or the United States. His job title: flavor chemist.

Evan Cattanach's job is "noser" for the 166-year-old Cardhu distillery in the Scottish Highlands. The firm produces twenty-five-dollar bottles of single-malt whiskey. Cattanach shows up at bars worldwide to catch a sniff of his company's whiskey to make sure that each batch is correct. Cattanach's nose is insured for $1 million. His usual method is to rub several drops of whiskey on his hands, let the alcohol evaporate, and then sniff for the maltiness and earthiness that can be produced only in his homelands. Moreover, there are 75 other whiskey sniffers in Scotland—one for each distillery. Worldwide, there are about 150 people who have a sensitive enough nose to hold a job like Cattanach's.

*   *   *

David Shenk baby-sits cows in the lush farm country of Pennsylvania. The job is also known as relief milking. Shenk fills in for dairy farmers who go on vacation. Dairy cows can't just be ignored, because serious infections can set in if the cows aren't milked on time.

Donald Marlowe, with the Federal Food and Drug Administration in Rockville, Maryland, is the nation's chief condom tester. He does his work by putting condoms on a machine that inflates them with air to the bursting point, often at the size of a watermelon. Instruments then record if the condom was up to United States government standards for strength when it broke.

Yearly, almost thirty million imported condoms are rejected while about three million domestic condoms are recalled from store shelves. Some brands are routinely damaged at the factory, so Marlowe must be on the lookout for damaged brands as well.

A different kind of protection may be needed when visiting the creations of Leonard Pickel, a haunted house architect in Dallas, Texas. Pickel's firm, Elm Street Hauntrepreneurs, designs houses that scare the daylights out of people. Pickel says he's designed over a hundred haunted houses in the fifteen years since he created his first, a haunted room at college. Pickel moved on to designing haunted houses for Halloween fund-raisers for the March of Dimes in Dallas. That was when he perfected his basic principle, the Pickel Theory of Haunted House Design. He creates scary spaces by designing ghouls and beasts who come at you unexpectedly through ceilings, walls, and floors, and then vanish again. He has designed haunted houses for Six Flags Over Georgia, Astro-World, Six Flags Over Texas, and others. The lion's share of his work is special houses for Halloween, which are torn down after the holiday. From November through September, Pickel works on designs for new, scarier haunted houses.

"My basic task in designing haunted houses is reversing what's typically taught in architecture schools," Pickel says. "Normally, you conceive a room that people want to stay in. But I design rooms from which people want to flee. I use 'high-startle, low-gore' guidelines. I don't like to scare people with a lot of chop and blood. However, the houses are scary enough that we recommend children under twelve and people with heart problems not go through. I also design in a lot of emergency exits from the houses in case the experience gets too intense. That way, people can easily bail out if they get too frightened."

Perhaps it is this merciful touch in Pickel's haunted houses that has prevented his being visited by a hired revenge specialist. Scott Haire and two partners operate Hate, Inc. in Arlington, Texas. If you really can't express your feelings with a card, Hate, Inc. will deliver one of three "Spite-o-grams" to whomever you wish. They offer a heart-shaped satin box filled with rocks nestled in candy wrappers; a bouquet of dead, thorny black roses; or, their most popular offering, a ribbon-wrapped box containing a dead fish resting on a bed of tissue. Most of Hate, Inc.'s deliveries go out as practical jokes on Valentine's Day. And with General Motors threatening to close one of its plants in Arlington at the time of this writing, Hate, Inc. should be doing better business than ever before.

Another firm, Enough is Enough, in Newton, Massachusetts, has the motto, Creative revenge for today's world. They will deliver revenge in the form of one dead fish for whatever reason. Or, if you want a former special someone to get the idea you're fully aware there is more than one fish in the sea, Enough will send three smaller but equally dead fish. In the company, the order is known as "Stinkers from the Deep." The firm will also send a very stuffed shirt; a kit of instant coffee, creamer, sugar, and a cup labeled "Get Your Own Damn Coffee!"; a Sit-On-It-Cactus; and an empty champagne bottle with two used glasses in a box labeled "The Party's Over." The firm also offers a puffed-up, mounted blowfish that says: "Blow It Out Your Ear."

A chick sexer examines baby chickens and turkeys and separates them, because the sexes are fed differently. According to the Dictionary of Occupational Titles, the task is done by "turn-ing back the skin fold of the external cloacal opening or inserting an illuminating viewer into cloaca to observe the genitals." People who work in the trade say the job often results in eyestrain.

Another animal-related job is foster parent for companion monkeys. South American capuchin monkeys are placed with quadriplegics after they have been trained through a program known as Helping Hands: Simian Aides for the Disabled. The clever, dexterous monkeys literally become helping hands for people who no longer have use of their fingers. Once trained, the monkeys can fetch, turn pages of a book, put a videocassette tape into a player, open a microwave oven, and even learn to comb a person's hair. But for the first five years of their lives, the monkeys must get used to living with humans in a home. After a nine-month application process, Dick and Misty Stewart of Phoenix, Arizona, became foster "parents" for Andy, a capuchin monkey who will someday become the hands of a quadriplegic. There are thirty-nine other foster parents like the Stewarts. Cur-rently, about twenty monkeys like Andy are already living with, and helping, quadriplegics.

"The monkeys are just like little people," says Dick Stewart. "They are funny at times and have temper tantrums at times. Raising one is just like having a human baby in the house." After five years, the monkeys leave their foster parents and go through a one-year training course to learn all the chores they need to know for living with a quadriplegic.

Some jobs seem so distasteful that workers *MUST* be doing them for the money alone.

For instance, deodorant companies employ odor judges who sniff all manner of armpits, both with and sans the firm's product.

An outhouse cleaner travels to construction sites with a pump truck and empties the holding tanks of portable privies. The job gets trickier when the toilet is kept many stories above ground on high-rise projects. (A contractor saves money when his high-paid workers don't have to make a major journey going to the john or jane.) In such a case, the outhouse is first lowered by crane down to the pump truck.

Another bathroom job, toilet flusher, was created in 1989 when the city of Jackson, Florida, hired twenty-three people to work an unexpectedly cold weekend before Christmas doing nothing but flushing the 503 toilets at the Gator Bowl to prevent the water pipes from freezing.

But perhaps the ultimate bathroom chore is found in canine sanitation. Some businesses dedicated to the dual propositions of clean yards and unsoiled sidewalks arrange for a professional pooper-scooper to visit homes with dogs and clean the yard weekly or bi-weekly.

Another sometimes-nasty job that *SOMEBODY* has to do is in the Office of Currency Standards in the Bureau of Printing and Engraving in Washington, D.C. When United States bills have been trashed beyond recognition, an inspector there looks over the cash, decides how much was probably there in the first place, and then replaces the cash with a government check. For instance, years ago, a farmer stashed some extra cash in the barrel of his shotgun, forgot about it, and then blew away the bills when he went hunting. The farmer sent what was left to the Office of Currency Standards for an examiner to look over, or through. Another farmer lost his wallet, which had contained $600. His only clue was that the wallet had been eaten by one of his cows. The farmer slaughtered the animal and sent its stomach—because some bills were plastered to the lining of the organ—to the currency examiners, who were able to recognize and account for $473. Other currency has been sent in from plane and car crashes, or thick with mold because the cash had been buried for many years. One of the largest cases involved sorting out thousands of bills worth several million dollars from an armored car that caught on fire and exploded.

*   *   *

More and more specialized areas seem to be available for police officers. While everybody has seen a traffic or motorcycle cop, there are also officers who police the art world, canals, restaurants, and even fruit orchards.

Detective Joe Keenan, of the New York Police Department's Major Case Squad, specializes in stolen art and art fraud. The only other art cop in America is Los Angeles Police Department Detective William Martin. On one case, Detective Martin came across a dealer trying to sell a Renoir, *Young Girl with Daisies*, for around $3 million. Martin knew the original was worth $10 million and was hanging in the Metropolitan Museum of Art in New York. That arrest led to the recovery of $15 million worth of counterfeit prints.

The California Aqueduct flows south five hundred miles from the Sacramento River delta to provide southern California with most of its drinking water. Last year, there were seven drownings in the canal, which ranges from eighteen to thirty feet deep and up to eighty feet wide. Moreover, the following items were dumped there: forty stripped and stolen cars, a stolen sheriff's car, a safe, countless guns, computers, shopping carts, several bodies, and a telephone booth. The canal cops patrol the length of the aqueduct with small planes equipped with large loudspeakers. Mostly, they chase away trespassers who want to fish or swim. One trespasser brought his water skis and was being towed in the canal by a car driving along the canal's frontage road. Fifteen officers and three light planes make up the canal patrol.

In Portland, Oregon, "StyroCop" Lee Barrett travels around the city checking into complaints on restaurants using outlawed polystyrene foam fast-food containers. (Polystyrene was banned because its manufacture damages the ozone layer. And Portland has declared the nineties the "Green Decade.") Although Barrett is not a police officer, he enforces the plastic foam ban by issuing a summons and fine to restaurants handing out food in the forbidden material.

Sheriff deputies work as "Avocops" in Ventura, Santa Barbara, Riverside, San Diego, and other counties of California where avocados are grown. Yearly, the avocado crop is worth anywhere from $185 to $200 million, but middle-of-the-night thieves sneak off with as much as $10 million worth. Avocado policing means a lot of night work in the field, groves, and orchards. While waiting for fruit thieves in the dark, some cops have learned to hear the difference between a piece of fruit falling to the ground and a ladder being set down. San Diego County sheriffs have three full-time detectives detailed to patrol against avocado theft. Grand theft, avocado—stealing over one hundred dollars worth of fruit—can net a thief six months to a year in jail.

Yet another kind of policeman carries no badge at all. "Diet cops" are weight-loss specialists who organize programs for figure-conscious clients. Extremely popular with actors and sports players, diet cops will police their clients' eating habits by bursting unannounced into their clients' kitchens and raiding their pantries to check for outlawed foods. One diet cop has a client with a weakness for sweets so she, the cop, calls a restaurant when her client is there and asks the waiters to skip driving the dessert cart by his table. Diet cops will also strip a client's workplace fridge of banned treats and replace them with something lower in calories.

Another food-related job is food stylist. That's a person who works with photographers to make sure ads featuring foods are as mouth-watering as possible. The food stylist's bagful of tricks includes gluing almonds onto muffins, gluing sandwiches together with a clear caulk, and pouring cooking oil over day-old fried eggs to make them look as if they had just come off the grill. Ice cream can be photographed under hot lights for hours on end because a food stylist is standing nearby blasting the dish with a can of freon. Stale hamburgers spring instantly to juicy life when brushed with soy sauce and water.

*   *   *

A sagger preparer and roll repairer don't work in plastic surgery, nor does a wrinkle chaser go to medical school. And a bone crusher is not necessarily always found in alley fights.

A sagger preparer has nothing to do with making people look younger. The occupation is found in the pottery industry where a "sagger" is a box or case that holds the finer ceramic wares while they are baking. A roll repairer works in a refining plant, repairing the machinery that transports and processes ore. While everybody over forty has probably wanted to chase a wrinkle or two, a wrinkle chaser works in a shoe factory and irons wrinkles from shoes or shoe parts. The bone crusher is not a bouncer or a boxer, although some pugilists have had that nickname. That person tends machinery that crushes animal bones used to make glue.

The World Future Society (WFS) studies current directions and trends and makes projections of the types of jobs and occupations that will be needed by the year two thousand. According to the WFS, occupations needed in the near future could include:

- Space recreation specialist. With more people entering and living in outer space, there will be a large need for relaxation and new games to play during free time. Games will be played differently because of low, or no, gravity.
- Space physician. The human body functions differently in outer space than on earth. For instance, when astronauts come back to earth, they are about two inches taller, and their legs are weaker because human bones lose calcium when they are away from gravity. Even the heart is enlarged and operates differently. So doctors must learn a whole new field of medicine.
- Moon geologist. This specialty will entail study and work with the moon just as geologists now study and interpret earthly formations. An exobotanist will work with plants

that are grown on the moon or on ships traveling into deep space while an exobiologist will work with all sorts of living systems which have been moved into outer space.

- Lunar miner. Mines will be set up on the moon and on asteroids to extract their precious minerals and ship them back to earth.
- Thanatologist. Here on Earth, more people will continue living into what is known as hyper-old age. And, as AIDS and other diseases spread, there will be more need for professionals to counsel and comfort the terminally ill.
- Holographic inspector. That's a person who will scan products just off the assembly line and compare them with a 3-D version of the perfected master product stored in a computer.
- Orthotists. As high-tech wizardry becomes more advanced, artificial limbs will be able to do more things for more people. The orthotists will specialize in bionic limbs and fitting such prostheses to patients with deformities or amputations.
- Electric car mechanic. Futurists say the era of the internal-combustion-engine car is limited because of the pollution it creates. By the year 2,000, there could be as many as ten million electric cars on the road. Those vehicles must have their batteries recharged often, and service stations will spring up to recharge and repair the cars.

7
SPORTING SILLINESS

Since the turn of the century, many Olympic events have disappeared, usually for good reasons. At various points in Olympic history, the competitions have included deer and pigeon shooting, club swinging, kayak slalom singles, rope climbing, the tug-of-war, the plunge for distance, motorboat racing, polo, cricket, golf, croquet, roque, and pistol dueling.

The oldest competitor ever to win a medal in the Olympics was seventy-two-year-old Oscar Swahn, who took a silver medal in the 1912 Olympics for the deer shoot, according to Olympic expert Andrew Strenk. Swahn had also won a medal in the same event in the 1908 Olympics.

Moving targets—not live deer—were used in the last Olympic deer shoot, which was held in Melbourne, Australia, in 1956. But in the 1900 Paris Olympics, live birds were used for the pigeon-shooting event. A flock of birds would be released in front of a participant with a shotgun; the winner was the one who knocked the most birds from the sky. Leon de Ludent of Belgium won the gold medal that year by knocking down twenty-one birds.

But pigeon shooting with live birds turned out to be a rather messy event. There were maimed birds on the ground and bloody feathers swirling in the air. The live-pigeon shoot was dropped and replaced by trap shooting, which uses clay pigeons.

In the pistol-dueling event, participants fired not at each other but at targets twenty to twenty-five meters away. That event appeared only once, in the 1906 Olympics in Athens. Other discontinued shooting events include miniature rifle teams (the rifles, not the contestants, were miniature), military rifles, free rifles, small-bore rifles, and military revolvers.

The defunct plunge for distance began with a standing dive from a platform. The diver was allowed a single leg and arm kick to propel himself underwater, away from his point of entry. The dive was measured after sixty seconds—or when the contestant's head broke the surface, whichever occurred first. "It was how far you went and how long you could stay down," Strenk says. The plunge for distance was held only once, at St. Louis in 1904. Americans garnered all three medals.

Held in the six Olympics from 1900 to 1920, the tug-of-war was a popular but contentious event. Its rules were simple enough—the first team to pull its opposition six feet won. If five minutes of tugging passed and one side was not pulled the required distance, the team that had moved its opponents the farthest won. The 1908 Olympics in London saw a tug-of-war that turned into a near riot when the United States team was beaten in the first round by a team of Liverpool cops who later took a silver medal in the event. The Yanks vigorously protested because the Brits were wearing boots with steel cleats, spikes, and heels. The protest was curtly overturned and the United States team, miffed, withdrew.

"In the tug-of-war, there was always controversy," Strenk says. "During one Olympic tug-of-war, spectators jumped over the fence and helped their respective teams pull. Fights broke out and the situation deteriorated into a riot."

An event that caused no rioting, though, was club swinging. Held in the 1904 and 1932 Olympics, it involved juggling, not bashing. The clubs resembled small bowling pins; the contestant had six minutes to do his or her routine. But the clubs could not touch each other or any part of the performer's body, other than the hands.

The last participant to win the rope climb was American Raymond Bass, in 1932. The rope climb was a timed event, with six or seven seconds considered fast. Bass went on to real fame in World War II for being the only submarine commander to take his sub in and out of Tokyo Bay during the war and live to tell about it.

Several forms of croquet—singles, doubles, and two-ball— were played in the 1900 Olympics. The winners in the motorboat event won by chugging along at about fifteen miles an hour in 1908, the last year that event was held. Polo was played five times between 1900 and 1936, while lacrosse was included in the 1904 and 1908 games.

There's nobody alive today to tell about Olympic cricket, which was last played in 1900. The event was dropped because of the pressure brought on the Olympic Committee by the many countries who complained that the British teams always seemed to have an advantage.

You don't have to go back into history to find sports which are not exactly household words.

Take underwater hockey, for instance. Governed by the Underwater Society, the sport is played by forty United States city teams and in about a dozen other nations. There are yearly playoffs to pick the best United States team, and then international competitions. In 1991, San Francisco held the title for best city team in the United States, while the Australian underwater hockey team was tops worldwide. New Zealand was selected as host nation for the 1992 World Championships. For a while, there was a move afoot to include underwater hockey in the International Olympics.

Also known as "Octopush," underwater hockey was started

in 1954 by British scuba divers who needed something active and fun to stay in shape during the winter months. They came up with a game based on hockey but played on the bottom of a swimming pool under at least twelve feet of water. The object of the game is for a team of six to push a two-pound brass puck into an opposing team's goal with puck-pushers that look like sawed-off shuffleboard sticks. Each player wears swim fins, a diving mask and snorkel, and one bulbous glove on his dominant hand to protect his knuckles from being scraped and ground on the pool's bottom. They can tell each other apart underwater because one team grasps black puck-pushers while the others hold white. They also wear swimming caps that match the color of the sticks.

Moving back and forth on the underwater playing field, the players must also reckon with moving up and down through many feet of water. So one of the most valuable assets for a player is "bottom time"—the time he or she can hold the breath while charging down the field pushing, or fighting for, the brass puck. Twenty seconds of bottom time is considered quite good in an active game. The goals are six-inch-high, four-feet-long metal troughs that sit at each end of the pool bottom. Even in the noiseless world of underwater hockey, the puck makes a satis-fying—or disheartening, depending on which side you're on—CLUNK! when it slides into the goal.

Underwater hockey playing "fields" can be very different, depending on the pool you're in. Rules say the pool should be about seventy-five feet long by about thirty-six feet wide. Some pools have tile bottoms so the puck zips along farther and faster. (A hearty shove will send the puck about ten feet on a concrete bottom.) Not all pools offer exactly twelve feet of water so depth varies between six and seventeen feet. Some facilities have a sloping bottom which can mean an uphill fight at times.

A few pools have underwater viewing ports, so the action can be filmed or televised. That's important if you're a spectator. Most first-time viewers are struck by the game's ballet-like movement as players pirouette around and around the puck while others seem to reach, kick, and race in three-quarter time, their movement slowed by the drag of the water.

A similar sport, underwater rugby, is also played with six players in—or under—the water. The ball is filled with salt water and doesn't float. The goals sit eighteen inches from the pool bottom and look something like an open-wire wastebasket. A game is begun when one of the water referees places the ball in the center of the field on the pool's bottom. Each team lines up along the pool edge at its respective end. At the sound of a whistle, all go for the ball. The ball is then passed toward the opponent's goal as quickly as one can throw a heavy, ten-inch ball underwater. The goalie may defend the goal but can't put his body over the basket to prevent a score. Unlike underwater hockey, the goalie remains back by his goal, trying to coordinate his need for air with defense. The teams tell each other apart because one side wears black wristbands and caps while the other wears white.

Yet another form of hockey is played in Pasadena, California, by workers at the Jet Propulsion Laboratory. Unicycle hockey is played on a basketball court, using unicycles to move around and lengthened ice-hockey sticks to flip a puck up and down the court and into the goals.

A sister sport, bicycle polo, began in Colorado, where players use the popular fat-tired mountain bikes. The sport is now played in six nations and is governed by the World Bicycle Polo Federation. It is often known as "poor man's polo"; one of the first rules provided for no intentional contact between riders. But everybody wears helmets, anyhow. Otherwise, the game is played almost the same way as regular polo. While furiously pedaling your bike and ignoring one of the brakes—because you must also hold the mallet—you strike a plastic ball downfield toward the opponents' goal. There are four players to a side and only two opposing players at a time are allowed to play the ball at a given moment. During the game, most riders travel parallel to the sidelines and have a right of way of four bike lengths in front and three feet on either side.

Another bicycle-based sport is cyclocross, a combination of running, cycling, and lifting. Cyclocrossers use sturdy mountain bikes and special cyclocross bikes to get through a dirt course filled with ditches, gulleys, hills, trestles, fences, logs, and other barriers. The timed event is basically steeplechase on wheels, so you must dismount and carry your bike many times during the course.

While many golfers are known for their perseverance, one golfing event is sure to test their passion for the game.

The annual Pioneer Pass Golf Challenge is billed as the world's longest and toughest tournament. Players gather at the top of a seven thousand-foot mountain to start what can be best described as cross-country golf. The "course" is twenty-seven miles long and ranges through a wilderness pass where sheer cliffs, ravines, endless mountain meadows, and even snakes menace the players. Golfers arrive equipped with four-wheel-drive vehicles and three or four spotters to pinpoint exactly where the ball lands in the rough territory.

Pioneer Pass is about 35 miles north of Palm Springs and about 110 miles east of Los Angeles. The tournament starts near Big Bear Lake, a ski resort in the San Bernardino Mountains, and is played down to the desert floor. "Holes" on the course are twenty-foot circles chalked on the ground around boulders, sagebrush, standing and fallen trees, rattlesnake-nesting rock piles, and, in one case, a body of water.

Hazards are a bit more creative. While most of the course is a gigantic sand trap, there are also cacti like the incredibly sharp Spanish Bayonet, cliffs, abandoned mine shafts, wild burros, and off-road motorcyclers who have ground more than one golf ball into the dirt. Despite these hazards, the tournament is popular enough to have been played for thirty-one years.

"It takes a hardy person to play Pioneer Pass," says Pat Toy of Yucca Valley, California. "Often, a tee-off spot will be cleared on the side of a hill. You stand there like a mountain goat trying to swing. Then, after you've finished a hole, it's very rough country to the next tee. I thought they were absolutely NUTS when I first heard about the tournament twenty years ago, but now I wouldn't miss it for anything!"

The Pioneer Pass Tournament started in 1959 when the citizens of Yucca Valley began agitating for a more direct paved road to the mountain ski resorts, fifty-one miles away by highway. To publicize the need for a shorter, paved road, thirteen community leaders decided to play a game of golf UP the pass. They strapped their golf bags onto their horses and camped out at night as the three-day "tournament" took them up the mountain.

But while the public demand for a short, paved road to the ski areas eventually faded, wilderness golfing through the pass quickly caught on. The event is now organized by Blue Skies Country Club in Yucca Valley, California, each September, and a player's wilderness score is combined with eighteen holes of regulation golf, played the next day on ordinary grass links.

Rules in the wilderness portion are naturally a bit different than for country club golf. Each player is assigned a judge/scorekeeper. Most golfers enlist spouses, children, and friends to serve as spotters and forward observers. More than once, a golf ball has wedged itself in the crotch of a tree, disappeared down a rabbit or gopher hole, or flown beyond reach over a cliff. Each player is issued five numbered balls and is charged one stroke if any are lost. Because the ground is so rough, players are allowed to tee up for every shot; many use spent shotgun shells. And because your ball is likely to land in the most impossible situation, you're allowed to move it for your next shot up to six club lengths in any direction NOT toward the hole.

At the other end of the thermometer, there's the Bering Sea Ice Golf Classic in Nome, Alaska, played every March. Because of all the ice and snow, orange golf balls are used, and sunk in flagged coffee cans. Despite the bright color, many balls are lost amid ice chunks in the Bering Sea.

On one of the longest days of the year, the Friday closest to June 21, the Yellowknife Golf Club in Yellowknife, Canada, holds the Midnight Golf Tournament in honor of a sun which never quite sets; tee-off is at midnight. The event ends at 6 A.M. the next day. While the tournament is played mostly in light, organizers say it gets somewhat dusky for twenty or thirty minutes around 12:30 and then gets light again.

The Yellowknife tournament contains one of the oddest hazards found anywhere: pesky, strong ravens that love to steal golf balls, even before they stop rolling. Recently, while the Yellowknife fire station roof was undergoing repairs, workmen found a cache consisting entirely of balls the birds had filched from the golf course.

In the Pillar Mountain Golf Classic, held in Kodiak, Alaska, duffers play one hole up a fourteen-hundred-foot mountain. Included in the bag with woods and irons are heavy duty tools to clear away brush, snow, and ice for each shot; however, no chain saws or motorized vehicles are allowed. Of the tournament's earnings, 50 percent goes to a local hypothermia unit.

Disc golf is about as far away from regulation golf as you can get. Instead of using woods, irons, and balls, you use Frisbees. The idea is to fly a Frisbee from tee to "hole" with as few strokes, or flights, as possible. There are about 240 disc golf courses worldwide. On natural courses, the "green" is a pole with tape at the top and bottom. Strike the pole between the taped marks and the "hole" is completed. On championship courses, the Frisbee must be flown into a metal basket. Over the basket are light chains, hanging from an umbrella-like device, that help deflect the disc down into the basket.

The Great International Klondike Outhouse Race is held in Dawson City, Canada, every year in September. For the last fifteen years, teams of five have constructed an outhouse that must look something like your standard farmyard privy, have a door with a moon-shaped hole or some other type of window, and a sloped roof. Four entrants push or pull their outhouse over a 1.8-mile course that travels over hills and rough ground, through mud and narrow places. The rules say that one team member must ride inside the outhouse during the race. Recently, the winners pushed their entry, "White Lightning," over the course in a blistering nine minutes, forty-three seconds—thirty-four seconds faster than the previous winner's time.

Of course, one of the most popular and simplest athletic activities of all is running. But the unusual variations that humans have devised for such a basic pursuit are many.

The Backward Mile Race is held in New York City every April Fool's Day. The participants celebrate the spirit of backwardness by facing to the rear while running. Typical winning times for the reverse miles: seven to eight minutes.

Then there's a running game known as hashing. Reportedly, the game was invented in Malaysia in the 1930s by bored Australians and Englishmen suffering through back-water diplomatic assignments. Back then, one runner was designated the Hare and given a twelve-minute head start. His or her task was to lay a six- or seven-mile trail through the jungle with torn bits of the *Malaysia Mail*, the only English-language reading matter then available. But the Hare added a twist—he broke the trail in three or four places and marked it with a big X. Somewhere within several hundred yards of the X, the trail would be clearly marked again and lead on through the jungle. Thus, the slower runners easily stayed up with the faster ones because the first runners down the trail had to do all the searching. Then, after the race, the runners met at a favorite restaurant, the Hash House, for dinner and copious libations to quench their collective jungle thirst. The restaurant became inextricably associated with the game, and thus the sport of hashing was born.

Today, the various hashing chapers are known as the Los

Angeles Hash House Harriers, the Seattle Hash House Harriers, and so on. The sport is rich with tradition and pranks, so wily Hares lay their trails through poison ivy patches, brambles, mud, cacti, and, in one case, "barbed wire strung at birth control level." So it's not entirely unusual for a runner to get lost on a hash.

One hashing custom is for one of the faster runners to carry a bugle. When the trail is found again after one of the X-marked breaks, the runner-bugler blows some flat, bleating notes on the instrument, alerting everybody that the trail has been relocated and that the runners are again running—instead of stumbling around looking. Surrounding runners then cry "On! On!"

The sport's only fatality happened when a 1950s-era Hare stumbled over an Indonesian waterfall while marking a trail and landed on his machete. Another time in the 1950s, during Malaysia's communist insurrection, a group of hashers ran eagerly down a not-so-clearly-marked trail and rousted a camp of sleeping guerrillas. The runners scattered, the guerrillas went for their rifles, and one hasher went for the police. Most of the guerrillas were arrested by troopers who chose to ignore the hashers' paper trail and find their own way.

Today, in environmentally correct times, hashing trails are laid through cities with chalk and through the countryside with flour. The sport's sometimes corny traditions call for the club treasurer to be known as the "Hash Cash," the newsletter editor, the "Hash Trash," the club photographer, the "Hash Flash," the first aid person, the "Hash M*A*S*H*," and so on. During any one run, there is virtually always a Beer Check—sweating runners can take their pick of beer, water, or soft drinks. Moreover, any occasion can be celebrated with a special hash—there are wedding, birthday, and anniversary hashes, and hashes with special themes, like the annual miniskirt hash (in California, of course). Even male participants must run in a mini. At last count, there were about 142 American hashing chapters.

High-Rise Staircase Running takes place in cities that have an abundance of tall buildings. The race starts on the first floor of a skyscraper and goes to the top. Racers are allowed to use gloves because grabbing onto staircase handrails is legal. Fastest time wins.

An outside staircase race was once held in Muelenen, Switzerland, where the world's longest staircase is located. Mount Niesen, in the Swiss Alps, has 11,674 steps, six times as many as the Empire State Building. Concrete, wood, and metal steps lead to an elevation of 5,300 feet and are used to allow maintenance workers access to a cable railway. The winning time: fifty-two minutes, twenty-six seconds.

K-9 Couples Running combines a jogger with a canine companion who faithfully trots alongside. Distances vary, and dogs must be as conditioned as their masters and mistresses. Over any course, the four-legged runners are usually distracted by fire hydrants, stray cats, and other dogs. Human runners often say the K-9 races are something like running through a forest of leashes.

One offbeat sport has presidential origins. Hooverball was invented in 1929 to help President Herbert Hoover stay in shape. The thirty-first president, along with a group of men known as Hoover's "Medicine Ball Cabinet," played the game daily in Washington, D.C. In Hooverball, a six- or nine-pound medicine ball is heaved over a volleyball net by three-player teams. The scoring is the same as in tennis.

"Hooverball is sort of like throwing a frozen turkey back and forth over the garage roof," says one player.

An annual Hooverball tournament has been held on Hoover's birthday, every August 10 since 1988 at West Branch, Iowa, Hoover's birthplace and the site of the Hoover Library. The various teams across the nation are overseen by Herbert Hoover Presidential Library Association worker Scott Sailor.

When beep ball was invented in 1965, it consisted of a few vision-impaired children swinging a bat at a softball that beeped as it traveled through the air. But the sport has gained such popularity that an annual National Beep Baseball World Series is played. In some games, sighted players join in as well, wearing blindfolds so they too must play by ear. In beep ball there are six fielders, while the pitcher and catcher are from the same team as the batter; the idea is to let the batter hit the ball. Bases are three-foot-tall columns of foam with a speaker inside that makes a different sound than the beeping ball. The scorer turns on the beeper in one of the bases when the batter hits the ball. Second base was eliminated to prevent collisions. Because the game relies on hearing, fans have to cooperate as well and refrain from cheering until a play is over. Beep-ball players say their ball is more delicate than a softball, so many are used during a game.

Other sporting events call for competition between vehicles, with varying results.

Twelve Mile, Indiana, has sponsored the Twelve Mile 500 Riding Lawnmower Race on July 4 for the last twenty-nine years. During the race, riders are limited to twelve miles an hour in the front straightaway where grandstands and bleachers are filled with hundreds of fans. However, in the back straightaway, contestants run their lawnmowers as fast as possible, often somewhere near twenty-six miles an hour.

The Twelve Mile 500 consists of sixty laps around a quarter-mile track for a total of fifteen miles. Racers must qualify for their positions before race day and may only enter factory-built, stock riding lawnmowers. The race begins with a cry of "Gentlemen, start your mowers!" while the drivers stand next to their machines. The Twelve Mile 500 has had its share of mishaps, with engine fires leading the list.

Chain racing is a motorized sport in which three vehicles are hooked together. The main driver rides in the first car doing all the usual things, stepping heavily on the gas pedal, fighting the steering wheel, and shaking his fist at the other drivers. But another driver rides in the last vehicle to steer it so the chain doesn't go wildly out of control. The event is particularly hair-raising because in many places chain racers speed around figure-eight tracks.

The yearly Great Cardboard Boat Regatta in Sheboygan, Wisconsin, requires sailors to build a person-powered boat from corrugated cardboard. The craft must be capable of racing a two hundred-yard course four times. The rules prohibit application of any type of tar, glue, resin, or varnish to the vessels, so they frequently become waterlogged and sink. (Shrink wrap, duct tape, and plastic sheeting are also verboten.) Some of the soggy sailing craft in years past have been shaped like a Viking ship, a sidewheel paddle boat, the Flying Dutchman, an offshore racer, a tugboat, a pencil, a whale, a hydroplane, a pirate boat, a submarine, a sailfish, a tank, a gigantic lawnmower, and a Roman galley with a toga-clad crew. (The boats can be crewed by as many as ten.)

The most magnificent boat to sink receives the "Titanic Award." The most imaginative or best designed craft receives the Cardboard Coupe Award. The most sensational sinking of a boat receives the Edsel Award. The entrants who win the Edsel and Titanic awards have to really want them—their soggy craft must be salvaged and presented to the judges on dry land.

For those who are unorganized and can't plan very far in advance, the Cardboard Regatta has an "Instant Boats" class. Entrants receive a kit at the race site and have about two hours to put their boats together.

One water sport with a little more zip is barefoot water skiing, which first appeared in 1947. The American Barefoot Club was organized in 1961. At first, membership was reserved for barefooters who could stay on their feet for a minimum of one minute. The sport was quickly picked up by the Australians.

Today, a World Championship tournament is held every two years with entrants from eleven nations. The events—wake slalom, tricks, and jumping—are performed much like regular waterskiing. For instance, in the wake slalom, points are awarded for crossing your boat's wake as many times as possible in fifteen seconds. The crossings can be made on two feet, traveling front-ward or backward, or on one foot, facing rear or front. In barefoot ski jumping, the takeoff edge of the ramp is about eighteen inches above the water line. To qualify for barefoot competition, women must jump 35 feet and men must clear 50 feet. The current men's world record for barefoot ski jumping stands at 72.8 feet.

A few sporting events that are inspired by history require steeds. The Natural Chimneys Jousting Tournament has been held every year since 1821 at Grottoes, Virginia, and bills itself as America's oldest continuously held sporting event. Instead of knocking another armored horseman from his steed, the joust requires a rider at full gallop to spear a two-inch steel ring with his lance. The National Jousting Association in Gladstone, Virginia, has ten local groups and a Jousting Hall of Fame.

However, you can take part in the real thing at the Renaissance Pleasure Faire, a Devore, California, festival permanently set in the year 1591. Knights in full, ninety-pound suits of armor charge each other on horseback with wooden lances, trying to unseat their opponents. Often, the lances splinter, without dislodging either knight.

But the most dread moment of all is when a knight suffers a "blowout." That happens when the rider is unseated by the recoil of his lance striking the opposing knight. Jousters say the feeling is like being momentarily suspended in space as your horse gallops out from under you. The clattering crash to the ground is said to be worse than a strong frontal hit from a lance.

The Society for Creative Anachronisms offers instruction in such manly arts as sword fighting and fencing. Members of the society, who practice as many arts and crafts from medieval times as possible, use rattan swords when armies, all clad in realistic costumes, clash in mock combat.

All types of lizards are entered in the World's Great Lizard Race, held every Fourth of July since 1976 in Lovington, New

Mexico. Contestants range from a one-inch skink to an eighteen-inch-long iguana, and they race in six heats down an inclined sixteen-foot ramp across the finish line into a Plexiglass container. Says "Lord of the Lizards" John Graham, event organizer: "Trainers may prod the lizards with a feather, but if your lizard tries to eat another competitor, your entry will be immediately disqualified."

Graham speaks from painful experience. The first year the event was held, the slithering racers, with names like Lightning, Speedy, Lizardnardo, and Bad to the Bone, were caged too long and ate each other. The winner that year was the creature with the biggest appetite.

Other creatures are featured in still more spectator sporting events. The Sunday before Thanksgiving sees the Live Turkey Olympics at the Inn on Lake Waramaug in New Preston, Connecticut. Starting with the traditional "March of the Birds," the gobblers arrive in time-honored costumes like Pilgrim's garb or pioneer togs. However, a few nonconformists always arrive attired as jailbirds, in punk rock getups, or in sweat suits. Following the lighting of the torch, athletic events begin. There is a high jump, a contest to see which turkey can gobble up poultry feed the fastest, and a slalom race. The birds are guided through the slalom gates by trainers who gently tap the turkeys on their sides with sticks.

For twenty years, Spalding University in Louisville, Kentucky, has sponsored the Running of the Rodents just before the Kentucky Derby. One race theme was Patriotic America, so the racing rodents had names like Patrirat Missile, General Ratton, Rat, White & Blue, Susan B. Ratoney, Ratsy Ross, and so on.

Known as "The Most Exciting Two Seconds in Sport," the rats race once around an oval track that looks like a miniature Churchill Downs. Wagers are limited to twenty-five cents. The winning rat receives—and usually promptly devours—a garland and a loving cup made entirely of Fruit Loops. The winner is also installed in the Rat Hall of Fame and retires to the home of its trainer as a beloved family pet.

For those who view sport as a release from stress, there's the annual Hill Country Machine Gun Shoot, held on Memorial Day weekend several miles northwest of San Antonio in Helotes, Texas. With a choice of about one hundred automatic weapons like Uzi machine guns, Lahti anti-tank rifles, or the stalwart M-16 rifle or M-60 machine gun, two hundred participants shred old refrigerators, washing machines, cars, and other discarded appliances and vehicles with hundreds of thousands of rounds. Forty bullets, which can be fired in mere seconds, are sold for about ten dollars. Other rental machine guns included the World War II-era .45 Thompson machine guns, M-3 grease guns and the more recent 9-mm MAC 11s, Sten guns, and AK-47s, the assault rifles long favored by Soviet-bloc client states.

Another ballistic sport, this for lovers of old guns, is Cowboy Shooting, barely a decade old. Most participants come from the Single-Action Shooter's Society. They strap on their finest—and historically correct—old western duds, pick up vintage shooting irons, and shoot for points at bull-shaped metal targets and whiskey jugs. Most shooters tote along a six-gun, an early repeating rifle, and a shotgun to complete the Old West mystique. In some events, participants must shoot their way out of a saloon or a bank robbery, or walk down a trail looking for ornery bushwackers disguised as pop-up targets.

One barroom sport has its genesis in the United States space program. Years ago, NASA developed a Velcro suit for training astronauts in the brief moment of weightlessness that comes by diving an airplane and then sharply pulling out. The inside walls of those training planes were lined with strips of Velcro so a trainee could stick to the wall if he wanted to stay in one place. Now, the technology is used in a sport known as "Stick to the Wall or Die Human Bar Fly." The activity has moved from the fringes of space to the innards of a New York City nightclub where patrons don a Velcro suit, take a flying leap from a trampoline, and hit as high as possible on a Velcro-striped wall. The mark is never hard to judge because the contestant, even if upside down, clings firmly to the wall.

Perhaps the messiest sporting event of all is the annual Tomato War between Texas and Colorado. The event is held on a slippery battlefield at Twin Lakes, Colorado, 120 miles southwest of Denver. The event requires a good throwing arm because the object of the sport is to remove opponents from play with a direct tomato hit to a vital area. The last unsplattered contestant is declared winner. Some players, using a new strategy, wear two T-shirts and peel one off when hit. Recently, participants flung in anger about twelve thousand pounds of overripe vegetables for an entire day. The Tomato War was first organized by the Inn of the Black Wolf so Coloradoans could express their occasionally unfriendly feelings toward Texans who flock to Colorado each winter for skiing. The first such battle was organized by a "General OberTomato" who wanted a visa system installed at Colorado's borders to keep Texans out of the Rocky Mountains. But the Lone Star skiers still flock to the slopes. During the war, the Texans carve out a piece of ground known as "The Tomalamo" and defend it to the end, usually winning.

Proceeds from the Tomato Wars go to a Colorado wolf protection project.

8
UNTOLD HISTORICAL TALES

Almost everything we learned about Christopher Columbus in school was a myth.

Except for native Americans, just about everybody is celebrating the five-hundredth anniversary of Columbus's landing in the New World. But a lot of what we "know" about Columbus is not so, say scholars and historians. Among the more popular untruths about Columbus handed down through the years:

- The explorer had to fight the notion that the world was flat and his ships would sail off the edge.
- The names of his ships were the *Nina*, *Pinta*, and *Santa Maria*.
- Columbus discovered a new continent.
- He was the first European to reach the New World.
- He died a penniless man.
- Spain's Queen Isabella hocked her jewels to finance the journey.

Says William Fowler, professor of history at Northeastern University in Boston: "Had Columbus known the actual distance to China, he probably would never have set sail. The explorer made his calculations about the size of the earth from Greek data and was off by about 60 percent. He thought he was sailing about three thousand miles directly to China when the actual distance to that country was closer to ten thousand miles." The small ships of the fifteenth century simply could not carry provisions for a journey that long.

The flat Earth theory held sway among common folk during the Dark Ages and was still popular among peasants in the fifteenth century, but "Before 1492, virtually all lettered men and certainly all European navigators knew the Earth was round," says Gerald Weissmann, M.D., author of *They All Laughed at Columbus*. Adds Professor Fowler: "Anyone claiming that a ship would sail off the end of the world in 1492 would have been laughed out of court."

The tales about sea monsters weren't as terrifying as they seem—at least, to the sailors of the day. Seafarers described to chart makers whales they saw at sea, which then were depicted as sea monsters on the edges of some maps. Rich imaginations took over when others saw maps for the first time.

Columbus proposed to sail west across the "Western Ocean," as the Atlantic was then known, to reach the Orient. But, as we all know, the explorer didn't know the entire Western Hemisphere was between Spain and Asia. Thus, when he landed in the islands we now know as the West Indies, Columbus thought he had reached the outer islands of Asia. When he made land in the Americas, Columbus sent out emissaries to search for the Great Khan of China. In fact, the explorer went to his grave convinced he had discovered a short sea route to Asia. He persisted in his beliefs because he found gold among the natives and heard rumors of great empires farther inland. In reality, those empires were the Inca in Peru and the Aztec in Mexico.

Columbus was hardly the first European to reach the New World. The Vikings in the eleventh century and the Irish in the sixth century sailed to the North American continent. Thor Heyerdahl, a modern explorer and author of *Kon-Tiki*, is leading a research project which he says will prove that Columbus knew about the Viking journeys and settlements in Greenland during the eleventh century.

"Historians have a map drawn by Portuguese sailors before the time of Columbus showing the coastline of Brazil," says Archibald Lewis, professor of history at the University of Massachusetts at Amherst. Professor Lewis says Columbus himself had been on expeditions to Iceland, Greenland, and to what is now Hudson Bay. So people of the fifteenth century already knew there were northern and southern land masses to the west of Europe.

Twenty-five years after the death of Columbus, in 1521, Magellan circumnavigated the globe and proved that Columbus had been bumping into a new continent, not the outer islands of China.

"One of the most popular myths about Columbus was that there was only one voyage," says Dr. Weissmann. "Actually, Columbus organized and led four expeditions to the New World."

After the first voyage, Columbus was hailed as a hero. So, for the second voyage, all the great adventurers of the day signed on. But on the third voyage, Columbus's entire flotilla was shipwrecked and marooned for a year on Jamaica. Columbus was ill and old beyond his years during the fourth and final voyage. Dr. Weissmann thinks Columbus had Reiter's disease, a crippling type of arthritis that strikes the joints below the waist and would have made it hard for him to move around. Columbus was in so much pain that his sailors built a small shelter on deck for him because it was too painful for the famous explorer to go below decks.

Columbus first solicited the kings of Portugal, France, and England, but they would not hear of financing a sea voyage to China. "The Spanish monarchy was at the height of its power and wealth and could easily afford the expedition, so there was absolutely no need for Queen Isabella to sell her jewels," Professor Fowler says. "Where that romantic myth came from has been lost to history."

What history does retain, however, was that a Spanish town, Palos, had fallen into disfavor with the crown. As punishment, Palos was ordered to build and supply ships to Columbus. Which leads to yet another popular myth. . . .

"The actual names of the ships in the first expedition were not the *Nina*, *Pinta*, and *Santa Maria*," Professor Fowler says. "The ship on which Columbus sailed was known to the crew as *La Gallicia*. *Santa Maria* and *Nina* are nicknames." The ship known as the *Nina* was really the *Santa Clara*. *Pinta* was also a nickname, but historians say the ship's actual name has been lost.

Myth holds that Columbus died a penniless man. He was disillusioned and in some disgrace when he died, but he was not broke. After his third voyage, Columbus fell into great disfavor and was arrested and sent back to Spain in chains because he could not fulfill his promises of Oriental silk, gold, and spices.

Says Dr. Weissmann, who is also a professor of medicine and director of the Division of Rheumatology at the New York University School of Medicine: "If Columbus had been in better health, the world probably would have become smaller, sooner. Columbus was a master navigator and normally could bring a four-ship flotilla across the ocean in only twenty-one days. But often his eyes were red and inflamed, and he was partially blind."

Columbus was only fifty-four when he died. Twenty-five years after his death, the globe was circumnavigated. If he had been in better health, the great explorer might have sailed on around South America and found just how far it really was to the Orient.

Although Columbus did not discover America, "He did establish a permanent connection between the Old World and the New," says Professor Lewis. And that required a man of vision, conviction, courage, leadership, and determination.

*   *   *

Eel for Thanksgiving? That's a hint of what the first Thanksgiving, in 1621, was really like.

If we were true to the original occasion, the feast would be held in late September or early October. Instead of watching televised football games, a popular seventeenth-century game such as cudgels, where two players stood in one spot and beat each other with clubs, would be played. The first to bleed was the loser. And the first such holiday was not called Thanksgiving, but a "Harvest Home" festival.

"Historically speaking, the first Thanksgiving we've come to know, with a couple of token Indians and grim Puritans in black and white garb, is basically myth," says James Deetz, former director of the Lowie Museum of Anthropology at the University of California, Berkeley. Professor Deetz spent two decades excavating and establishing the Plimouth Plantation (Plimouth is the old spelling) in Massachusetts.

The Harvest Home festival started in the Middle Ages in Europe and was held whenever a bumper crop was brought in. Sometimes, the event was held as early as August, but the very latest was early October. Whenever it was held, the occasion was marked by food and merry-making. The first English settlers understood the word Thanksgiving not as a holiday, but as a day spent in church, praying.

The myth of the black-and-white-garbed Puritan arose because most people of the time were pictured in black—their Sunday finery—when their portraits were painted. Black was a very expensive dye in the 1620s, and it quickly faded to purple, making black garb the most expensive. The cheapest dyes, all taken from vegetables, were red, yellow, and green.

The first English settlers in America were actually lusty Elizabethans, a colorful lot who wore multihued capes, velvet vests with brass buttons, lace and quilted caps, and soft boots that today would be recognized as suede. Those fabled high-heeled shoes with large buckles were worn twenty years later in England and then only by the very rich. According to researchers at the Plimouth Plantation Library, inventories from the era reveal that church leaders even wore green and red underwear.

These first settlers were members of the Separatist church movement and called themselves "Saints." About sixty others who arrived on the Mayflower in 1620 were known as "Strangers." They did not live in log cabins. That form of housing was brought to America much later by settlers from Sweden who colonized what is now Delaware. The first English settlers lived in proper timber-frame homes with plank siding.

The "Saints" valued wit and humor, knew how to have fun, and drank goodly amounts of liquor. In fact, a weekly duty for every housewife was making beer. Hard cider and a liquor that tasted something like brandy were also commonly available. The "Saints" drank alcohol because they considered water to be bad for their health.

"It appears from court records of the time there was drunkenness and fighting," Deetz says. "While making the Atlantic crossing, the Puritans wrote they much bemoaned the fact their supplies were largely spent—especially the beer. So they rushed to make land. You could almost argue it was a beer shortage that made the Pilgrims land where they did in 1620."

Other documents tell of wife-swapping, divorces due to adultery, and many marriages wherein the bride was already large with child.

"Prudishness simply wasn't practical," says Cheryl Walker, professor of English at Scripps College. "People weren't allowed to live alone then so men, women, and children, some of whom were strangers, slept in the same room. Bathing was done in a large tub, probably in full view of the household, and once Plimouth Colony started thriving, there were cases of wife and child abuse and infanticide."

The main dish at the Harvest Home festival was not our

favorite, turkey. "We know about the lack of turkeys because when we excavated ten sites at Plimouth Plantation, only one turkey bone was found," Professor Deetz says. "But the records describe how the Indians taught the settlers to stomp in the mud and drive eels to the surface where they are easily caught by hand. Wild turkeys were, and still are, wily and very hard to bag." Turkeys became associated with Thanksgiving when Abraham Lincoln made the holiday a national one in 1863.

Cranberries aren't mentioned in the records at Plimouth until 1650, probably because it required too much sugar to make the bitter berries tasty.

The real treat for the English at the first Thanksgiving was venison. Local Indians, who outnumbered the English ninety to fifty, contributed five deer to the feast. In England, deer belonged exclusively to royalty and it was against the law for a commoner to eat deer meat. The feast was rounded out by goose, duck, rabbit, fish, and shellfish like clams and lobster. The tables were also graced with soups, meat pies, skillet-fried breads made of corn, dried fruit, and all kinds of wild berries. Researchers claim that the English settlers weren't fond of vegetables but that they did eat a lot of squash and pumpkin.

The celebration included singing, dancing, and shooting matches among the English with their heavy, clumsy blunderbusses and with the Indians, who showed their marksmanship with arrows. The English sang popular folk songs and organized wrestling matches.

One of the popular games of the day, stool ball, was probably the ancestor of today's cricket and perhaps baseball. One player threw a ball while another used a three-legged stool to hit and run to the seventeenth-century equivalent of bases. They played tug-of-war and caber tossing, or "pitching the bar." A log, often the size of a small telephone pole, would be thrown as far as possible. If no logs were available, huge boulders were used.

Gentler souls who didn't play stool ball or who found cud-

gels too rough played "pillow bashing," which we know today
as pillow fighting. You didn't have to draw blood to win in pillow
bashing.

The fifty English settlers who enjoyed the first Harvest
Home celebration were thankful just to be alive. The Mayflower
set sail with a complement of 101 in September 1620, spent two
months crossing the choppy Atlantic, and arrived in the area
north of Cape Cod in December with 102. There were two births
during the journey, but one infant died. Winter set in as soon
as the English arrived, and it was too late for planting. By spring,
harsh weather and illness had taken half the settlement.

But the bad luck was reversed by friendly Indians, and the
settlers produced a bumper crop the following fall.

The start of communism in the world caused by a sick
little boy?

One of the pivotal events of the twentieth century was the
Russian Revolution in 1917. Soon thereafter, communism spread
to other lands and helped cause the Korean and Vietnam wars,
an incredibly expensive arms race, and other tensions that held
the world hostage for half a century.

But how did a sick child help bring about the first communist
nation?

The boy was the only son of Nicholas II and Alexandra
Romanov, Russia's last royal couple. Alexis Romanov was born
with hemophilia, an inherited blood-clotting disorder that strikes
only males and can cause fatal bleeding with only a small bump
or scrape. The Romanovs were sick with worry because they
had already lost close relatives to the ailment. Moreover, hemophilia was so common among royalty it was also known as
the "blueblood disease" or "royal disease." Alexandra Romanov
was as desperate for her son as were members of the Spanish
royalty who put their hemophiliac sons in padded suits and even
padded the trees in the parks where they played.

After seeing Alexis on death's doorstep many times, Alexandra lost faith in doctors, who had been ineffective in treating him. Instead, she turned to the holy men and faith healers of the era. One particular Siberian peasant was said to have miraculous healing powers. So when Alexis suffered a particularly bad case of internal bleeding, Alexandra sent for the peasant, Grigory Rasputin.

Says Alex de Jonge in *The Life and Times of Grigorii Rasputin:* "Rasputin came to the sick boy's bedside and prayed fervently. Shortly thereafter, the bleeding stopped. After that, Rasputin prayed for, and laid hands upon, Alexis whenever the lad was ill."

It was reported that Rasputin once cured Alexis from a distance by sending a telegram and then praying so fervently he, Rasputin, almost passed out. Some court observers thought the self-appointed holy man usually stopped the lad's bleeding through hypnosis. Also, Rasputin's healing visits always came a few days after Alexis's injury, so the bleeding may even have stopped on its own. However he did it, Alexandra firmly believed the life of her only son rested in Rasputin's hands. The peasant could also talk Czar Nicholas out of his terrible headaches— sometimes over the phone. Whatever his medical methods were, Rasputin completely ingratiated himself with Russia's ruling couple and became a royal confidant.

Eventually, Alexandra insisted on Rasputin's help with affairs of state. In 1905, a partial revolution had taken place in the legislative assembly, the Duma. In September 1915, goaded on by Rasputin, Nicholas suspended the Duma. It was known that reactionaries—inspired by Rasputin and Alexandra—expected that an Allied victory in World War I would make it possible to kill constitutionalism in Russia. Thus the forces of the Russian Revolution, with the Lenin-led Bolsheviks ultimately coming to power, were set in motion.

During his lifetime, Rasputin was known as a man who represented the real soul of Russia. He came from a background of folk healers and was coarse and uneducated but close to God.

He also believed in the divine right of kings and in absolute power for the Czar of Russia.

Unfortunately, Rasputin had an immense sexual appetite and was said to have seduced cooks, maids, and other workers at court. Eventually, a rumor circulated that Rasputin had taken up with the queen while Nicholas was away on a political mission, and had become the real power running Russia. Citizens were outraged and more encouraged than ever to overthrow the monarchy. In 1916, a few desperate nobles assassinated Rasputin, who had become known as "The Mad Monk," but the damage had been done. The scandal was a major factor in the success of the Bolshevik October Revolution of 1917.

Aleksandr Kerensky, a Russian politician of the era, observed: "If there had been no Rasputin, there would have been no Lenin." And if there had been no hemophilia, there would have been no Rasputin.

One of the world's favorite sporting events, the International Olympics, is rife with myths. Among the more popular Olympic untruths are:

- Ancient Greek athletes competed for olive branches only.
- Everything came to a halt for the ancient games.
- Adolf Hitler snubbed Jesse Owens in the 1936 Olympic Games in Berlin.
- The torch-lighting ceremony is handed down to us from ancient Greece.
- The distance for the marathon race was set by an ancient runner traveling from Marathon to Athens. The runner then died.

Is there a marathon runner anywhere who does not thrill to the story of the ancient Greek Pheidippides? He was the dedicated courier who, legend says, ran twenty-six miles full-tilt to announce victory over the Persians at the Battle of Marathon in 490 B.C. He then collapsed and died of sheer exhaustion at the feet of his grateful king. Or so the story goes.

The only problem is, it didn't happen. The 26-mile, 385-yard length of today's marathon is not the distance from Athens to Marathon. It is really the distance from Shepherd's Bush Stadium in London to just outside the queen's bedroom at Windsor Castle. That length became standard in the 1908 Olympic Games.

Former University of Southern California history professor Andrew Strenk took a sabbatical in 1984 to do a year's worth of spade work in the official Olympic archives for the Los Angeles Organizing Committee. Strenk had previously covered the Moscow games in 1980 for the Armed Forces Network and was a radio reporter for the 1976 games in Montreal. After the '84 games, Strenk taught a college course, "History and Politics of the Olympic Games."

Strenk's real quest for Olympic truth began in the mid-1970s while he was studying for a master's degree at the University of Würzburg in Germany.

"I heard from firsthand sources that Adolf Hitler did not deliberately snub Jesse Owens," Strenk says. The athlete who may have been snubbed by the infamous dictator was Owens's teammate, Cornelius Johnson, who won the high-jump competition near the end of the games' first day. Hitler spent that day calling over the winners, all of whom happened to be Caucasian, to congratulate them. After Johnson's victory, Hitler and his entourage left—either because it was dusk or because Johnson was black.

"The next day, the International Olympic Committee told Hitler he would have to congratulate all winners or no winners," Strenk says. "So the winners' personal appearances with Der Fuehrer ceased. It was that very day Jesse Owens did so well and, of course, Hitler did not congratulate Owens or anybody else. Jesse Owens himself said many, many times he was never directly snubbed by Hitler." But some journalists noted the dictator said nothing to, or about, the amazing Owens and, thereafter, the story of the Hitler-Owens snub became self-perpetuating.

At the same games, the Nazis drummed up a piece of public relations puffery that is still revered as a hallowed Olympic ceremony. The lighting of the Olympic torch by the sun's rays in Greece—and its subsequent relay to the site of the games—was a Hollywood-inspired piece of gimcrackery devised by the talented filmmaker Leni Riefenstahl, who became famous that same year for her propaganda film about the Third Reich, *Triumph of the Will*.

Other myths handed down to us from ancient times include the yarns about Greek wars being halted every four years for the games; that participants were strictly amateurs; that some city-states tore down their walls for the games, and that winners were satisfied with a crown of olive leaves as their only purse.

"The early Olympic Games were part and parcel of religious ceremonies that included animal sacrifices, dramatic and poetic readings, singing, and incense-burning," Strenk says. "Athletic events were only one segment."

In ancient Greece, the Olympics were organized something like today's Grand Slam in tennis. The big four sites for the games then were Delphi, Corinth, Olympia, and Aegina. The idea of purely amateur athletics actually came about in the eighteenth century, when upper-class Europeans were considering starting the games of the modern era. The idea of purely amateur athletics was important then because only the rich had the time for sports; everybody else was too busy working twelve-hour days.

In fact, the ancient Greek athletes were handsomely paid and, providing they won, brought high honor back to their respective city-states. They were given pensions and homes and earned the same type of wealth and fame as today's top professional athletes. "Records reveal that Elis and Corinth supported athletes year round," Strenk says. "They lived at the expense of the state and trained in specially built gymnasiums."

Scholars tell us the games played in the ancient Olympics

sprung mostly from the practice and arts of war. Ancient contests included Greco-Roman wrestling, much like the modern version, and a type of boxing wherein the participants wrapped their hands with leather thongs. One of the most popular events on the ancient card was the pancratium, a violent and bloody free-for-all that often resulted in gouged-out eyes and torn-off ears. Other events included foot races, the javelin throw, and the long jump. "The longest footrace the ancient Greeks held was about three miles," Strenk says. "They would consider a race of twenty-six miles [our modern marathon] absolutely crazy."

The popular horse-race events were divided into about every classification possible. In addition to two-, four- and ten-horse-team chariot races, there were filly-only chariot, mule-only chariot, and other such divisions. "In the equestrian events, it's clear the ancients did a huge amount of betting—and cheating," Strenk says.

The ancient pentathlon was a premier event because it tested the skills most used in warfare—running, jumping with a heavy stone, boxing, wrestling, and the javelin throw.

Despite the enduring myths about Greek champions being satisfied with tokens like olive branch crowns, the ancients would have quickly adopted the quote mythically attributed to Vince Lombardi: "Winning isn't everything, it's the only thing." (What Lombardi actually said: "Winning isn't everything, but wanting to win is.") To finish second was to return home in disgrace. The ancients thought the glory in winning was that it elevated a mortal to the level of a god. Some popular sports heroes of the era had their likenesses carved in stone.

Because the ancient games were part of a religious ceremony, the four sites were off-limits to those who carried the tools of war. Ancient wars did not cease for the games but warrior-participants could obtain a safe-conduct pass that allowed them to traverse battlefields at night when the day's fighting was done. As Strenk notes, "The Peloponnesian War went on for forty-four years and contained no halt, whatsoever, for Olympic Games."

And although politics are not supposed to contaminate the
Olympic ideal, Emperor Nero of Rome, during the games of
A.D. 66, did his best to ruin that high-minded notion. At the
time, it was widely suspected that Nero did not have both oars
in the water. But all doubt was removed when he issued a decree
that a musical contest would be included in the games, entered
the contest himself as a poet and singer, and crassly declared
himself winner. Historians also noted that Nero entered a ten-
horse team in the four-horse chariot race, fell from his vehicle,
and was almost killed. Nonetheless, he declared himself winner
in that event, too.

The games were thought by many to have stopped in the
fourth century A.D. The truth is, the games never died completely. The world of the Olympics became a more dangerous
and less organized place when Huns, Vandals, and Visigoths
started raiding the cities of the Roman empire. Also, there were
major earthquakes that changed the courses of rivers and flooded
the game sites at Delphi and Olympia. Moreover, the ruler Theo-
dosius I declared an end to "pagan rituals" in A.D. 397, and that
included—in his mind, at least—Olympic Games. Historians,
however, note that the same decree was issued about every fifty
years, which implies the games went on, decrees and procla-
mations notwithstanding. Some contests were held from time to
time in various places through the ages. For instance, Olympic
events were held in Syria in 1456. In 1612, Robert Dover organized Olympic competition at the Cotswold Hills in England.
The games were also held sporadically among northern Europeans and the English for the next 250 years. The Greeks staged
their own Olympic revivals in 1859, 1870, 1875, and again in
1877. Nonetheless, most credit for starting the modern Olympics
goes to French nobleman Baron Pierre de Coubertin, who was
responsible for the 1896 games and served as International Olympic Committee president until 1925.

"Coubertin's motives were pure enough—to bring the peo-
ples of the world together in sport and friendship," Strenk says.

"But the real inspiration for reviving the Olympics was probably picked up while watching the English play the ancient games."

Buy the film rights to a war?

Hollywood has gone to incredible lengths to get the rights to good stories. But to acquire the rights to a war and have the exclusive right to film it—while the war raged?

It happened in 1914, when Mexican revolutionary Pancho Villa sold the film rights to his war to the Mutual Film Corporation. "Pancho Villa was always very publicity-conscious and thought a movie about his revolution in Mexico would be a good way to curry favor with American audiences," says Paul Vanderwood, professor of Mexican History at San Diego State University. "So when Mutual offered him twenty-five thousand dollars and a percentage of the profits for the film rights to his revolution, Villa quickly agreed. He needed the money for arms."

Because the cameras of the era were big and clumsy and could only film in daylight, Villa had to agree to no night fighting and to setting up his battles for the cameras.

"Villa was a well-known figure among Americans because his wife lived in El Paso, Texas," says Professor Vanderwood. "So he had been to the 'moving movies,' as he called them, and knew the power of film."

Pancho Villa's reputation among Americans was huge during the Mexican Revolution. Some influential people like William Randolph Hearst thought Villa was a hero and hoped the general would become president of Mexico. But there were still a few Americans who believed Villa was just a bandit.

The general was often pictured in American newspapers on the battlefield in dirty khaki clothes and baggy pants. So when the agreement with Mutual was made, Villa decided he would let Americans see him in something else. He dressed up in silver-trimmed sombreros and Spanish leather boots and appeared in front of the cameras as much as possible in fresh uniforms.

Mutual sent a special railway car equipped with a darkroom

and photographic equipment to Mexico. Many times, Villa's generals suggested a night attack but the Mexican leader stood firm on his agreement with the movie studio and ordered his soldiers to fight only in daylight. Once, when Federal forces were retreating, Villa observed it was getting dark and let his enemy get away.

During another battle, Villa's men surrounded a town that was a federal stronghold. The rebel artillery was readied while the ragamuffin soldiers prepared for the attack. But, alas, the movie cameras were not in position. So Villa held off for two hours until the cameramen were ready. When the attack finally began, the victory was recorded on film. After that, the Mutual camera operators sat in on Villa's war conferences with other staff.

"Many times, when Villa and his generals were planning tactics, the Mutual cameramen objected to the battle plans because the strategy would not suit the cameras," Professor Vanderwood says. "Each time, Villa ordered the plans changed."

Once, when Villa's soldiers were waiting in ambush for an expected federal charge, a cameraman actually became the commanding officer. Villa's troops set up machine guns where they thought the federals would charge. But the Mutual cameramen complained to Villa that he would not get any decent shots because the range of the machine guns was greater than that of the cameras. So Villa ordered his soldiers to hold their fire until the camera operator gave the word. When the enemy was close enough to capture the ambush on film, the cameraman ordered the rebels to open fire.

Another time, the Mutual staff told Villa they needed to film a shelling barrage to make the movie more realistic. So one night, Villa ordered his artillery aimed at a nearby hill where, Villa said, there was a federal outpost. When day broke, the cameras had been set up and the order was given to fire at the entrenched federals. Bodies could be seen hurtling skyward. Later, the technician who processed the film told everyone it was the best war footage yet. Eventually, one of the survivors told reporters the troops at the federal outpost were actually prisoners of war who had been marched to the hill at gunpoint.

Partly because of his new clothes, Villa became something of a camera hog and seemingly wanted more shots of himself than of the fighting. So, every time Villa changed uniforms, he sent for the cameraman. The operator tired of shooting so much footage of Villa and started filming the general with an empty camera. The head cameraman once told an assistant he had fooled the vain Villa with an empty camera but a Mexican who understood English was standing nearby and heard the remark. When Villa found out, he became so furious that he threatened to stand the camera operator up against a wall before a firing squad. Only the fact that the operator was American saved his life.

"When the film was finished, it was shown to Villa and his staff, in Mexico and in the United States," Professor Vanderwood says. "Villa liked it extremely well but it was a flop at the box office. Not much later, Mutual was absorbed by RKO and the Mutual stockholders started a fight over who owned the rights to the negative of the film. It disappeared and was never seen again. Scholars have looked for the film for years but haven't been able to locate a single trace of it. I spent some time in London looking through the British Film Institute and couldn't find even a small clip of it.

"Pancho Villa later fell out of favor with American audiences when he crossed the United States border and raided Columbus, New Mexico. But by the 1930s, the legend of Pancho Villa had grown tall again. When the story of Pancho Villa's life was told on film again, Wallace Beery played the part and the movie did extremely well."

Villa ended his days in the northern Mexican village of Parral and was never caught or punished for the raid on United States soil. He lived in Parral until 1923, when assassins shot him to death. In 1926, grave-robbers stole Pancho Villa's head, and the skull's whereabouts have been a mystery ever since.

*   *   *

When you speak ordinary English, your words and phrases form a living history exhibit. Phrases commonly uttered by today's speakers of English have come down to us over the ages from Roman soldiers, English peasants, seventeenth-century sailors, rogue gamblers, American colonists, African slaves, and others.

For instance, let's eavesdrop on a typical office conversation that is filled with history. The people talking may not know their words represent over two thousand years of phrasemaking. And sometimes, the phrases we use mean the opposite of what we're trying to express. But let's listen to Fred and George for a moment to see how the past has made our language more colorful.

"That Jones isn't worth his salt," says Fred, a supervisor. "That son of a gun should be more sincere about his work. That last project is dead as a doornail because Jones just would not get down to brass tacks."

Replied George, a supervisor in another department: "I used to think Jones was playing the devil's advocate, because he said he would get the job done, come hell or high water. When he worked for me, nobody could hold a candle to his work. But you're right—he's always at loggerheads with everybody else now. Or else he's involved in some kind of tomfoolery and makes a bedlam of his department. I don't want to steal your thunder, but I also think Jones's project is going to kick the bucket. And if that happens, there'll be the devil to pay! Somebody should take Jones down a peg or two."

"Why, I'll eat my hat if Jones lasts another week. I'll be happy as a clam when he leaves."

"And then he goes job hunting," Fred says, "and every employer in town gives us the third degree because he doesn't want a pig in a poke."

"Dead as a doornail?" "Steal your thunder?" "Worth his salt?" "Son of a gun?"

Where do these phrases come from? How can somebody be worth salt or steal thunder?

In Roman days, part of your pay was given in salt, then a valuable commodity. The Latin *salarium* ("the money given to the soldiers for salt") came to mean payment for services rendered. Today, the Latin *salarium* (from the Latin *sal* ["salt"]) shows up in the English "salary."

"Son of a gun" started when officers and sailors of seafaring nations took their women with them on long voyages. Births at sea became common. When a woman was having a difficult delivery, she was taken out to lie by the vessel's cannon. When she least expected it, the gun was fired, startling the laboring woman and giving her the necessary impetus to give birth to the infant.

"Sincere" came into the language when ancient Roman sculptors advertised their quality work as *sine cera* or "without wax." Shoddy sculptors then worked quickly and filled in the nicks, cracks, and other mistakes with wax which lasted only a short while.

"Dead as a doornail" was used in England in the fourteenth century the same way we use the phrase today. Then, a doornail was a metal plate on a wooden door. The plate, struck by the knocker so many times, was said to have no life at all left in it.

Brass tacks? In nineteenth-century rural America, a general store sold a little bit of everything, material included. Rather than get out a yardstick for every purchase, the merchants pushed brass tacks into their counters to mark yards. Then, instead of guessing at the length of material, they merely put it "down to brass tacks."

Devil's advocate? In ancient Rome, when a candidate for sainthood was represented at the pope's court, the *advocatus diaboli* ("devil's advocate") gave every possible argument against canonization. Speaking for sainthood was the *advocatus dei* ("God's advocate").

If our friend Jones really intends to get the job done "come hell or high water," he had better do it right the first time. The phrase actually refers to a ghastly execution reserved for seventeenth-century pirates. At Execution Dock in Wapping, England, pirates, like the notorious Captain Kidd in 1701, were hanged by their wrists in a pit at low tide and left exposed until three tides (the high water) had submerged them.

Why do we "hold a candle" to something else as a means of comparison? Among fifteenth-century gamblers in England, stableboys or servants were often paid a few pence to hold a candle behind the gambler during all-night games so he could see his cards. But when he lost all his money, other gamblers contemptuously remarked the man was no longer able to hold a candle.

The first loggerheads were long-handled instruments with large metal cups on the end that were used to melt tar over open fires. In naval battles during the Middle Ages, sailors heated pitch and tar in loggerheads and flung the contents at attacking ships.

Bedlam? Tomfoolery? Several centuries ago, the insane were considered a source of amusement at Bedlam Hospital in London. The carryings-on of inmates were exhibited for entertainment near the violently insane who, struggling and screaming, were chained to walls. Soon, vast confusion, noise, and din became known as "bedlam." The nicknames "Tom 'o Bedlam" and "Tom Fool" were used for favored inmates who liked playing to the audiences visiting Bedlam.

Steal thunder? English playwright John Dennis devised realistic thunder to accompany his play *Appius and Virginia* in 1703. But his work wasn't popular and closed early. A few nights later, Dennis saw a production of *Macbeth* and discovered his sound effects were being used in the scenes with the witches. He jumped up and cried out, "See how the rascals use me! They will not let my play run, yet they steal my thunder!"

Kick the bucket? The frame from which a freshly killed pig was hung in old England was known as a "bucket." If the pig thrashed about, it kicked the bucket. Also, during that time, a common form of suicide involved a distraught person who stood on an upside-down pail with one end of a noose tightly fastened to his neck and the other tied to a beam. His last act in this world was "kicking the bucket."

Having "the devil to pay" first referred to a very undesirable task. The original phrase, used by seventeenth-century sailors, was "The devil to pay and no pitch hot!" The "devil" referred not to Satan, but to the ship's longest seam, running from stem to stern just below the main deck. "Pay" was seaman's talk for putting caulking into the seam and covering it with pitch. The job was done by lowering a seaman over the side on a bos'n's chair with a bucket of hot pitch. As the pitch cooled, the work became harder and downright impossible when the material was cold.

If Jones is to be "taken down a peg or two," his status is lowered. In the British navy in the eighteenth century, a ship's colors were raised by a system of pegs, with the highest peg being the most honorable. If a flag was lowered a peg, its honor was reduced.

If Fred is really going to "eat his hat," it might contribute to cavities. In Colonial America, sugar was extremely expensive and was sold in small cone-shaped packages known as "hats."

Happy as a clam? The original phrase was "happy as a clam at high tide" because the mollusks can be dug up only at low tide.

The third degree? The highest order of freemasonry is the third degree, the Master Mason. Candidates for that rank had to pass rigorous tests with many questions.

"Poke" means "bag" or "sack" in regional dialects in the United States and England and is the word from which "pocket" comes. At county fairs a century ago, a common fraud occurred when a sharpster claimed he had—at a bargain price—a suckling pig in a burlap bag, when actually the poke contained a cat. But if the farmer was clever, he inspected the bag's contents, refused to buy a pig in a poke, and also "let the cat out of the bag."

9

ONE-IN-A-MILLION ENCOUNTERS

When Allison Forciea, a medical assistant, came into the examining room to look at a patient, she could not believe her eyes. There, tattooed on the right side of the man's chest was "Edie Jo," the name she was born with but had not used in twenty-eight years, since she was two years old. On the left side of the patient's chest was another tattoo, "George Jr.," the name of Allison's brother. Edi Jo had become Allison when she and her brother were adopted by another couple after her birth family fell on very hard times and broke up.

Allison momentarily forgot about the patient's lump and left the examining room to pull herself together. George Jensen had not noticed the surprise and distress on her face and continued waiting for an orthopedic surgeon to examine a lump on his shoulder.

While collecting herself, Allison told her supervisor about the patient's tattoos, how she was adopted, and the possibility that the patient could be her birth father. The supervisor suggested that Allison coolly go about the business of assisting with the exam and approach the patient later as he was leaving the Vallejo, California, clinic.

"I felt like I was on the outside watching all this," Allison says. "I knew I wanted to say something to the man, but I was afraid how he would react. I was nervous, anxious, and excited at the same time."

Allison waited until Jensen's examination was finished and approached him on his way out of the clinic. The lump on his shoulder had turned out to be nothing serious.

"May I speak to you for a moment?" Allison asked. Jensen said certainly, thinking the young medical assistant had some information about his case. The couple walked outside the building.

"Please don't think me weird," Allison said, "but have you ever been married before?"

Before Jensen could answer, Allison blurted: "To a woman named Lois?"

"Why, yes, to a Lois Rosencutter in Kansas," Jensen said.

"Well, Lois is my mother and I think you're my father."

Jensen and Allison were standing in a doorway that had a collapsible metal security gate. Jensen felt his knees going out from under him and grabbed onto the gate for support. His eyes started filling with tears.

"I don't know what to say, I'm so sorry about everything, I just don't know what to say," said Jensen.

"How about hello?" Allison said.

Twelve years before, when Allison and George junior came of age, their adoptive parents gave them what little information they had about their natural parents. Allison managed to track down her mother in 1985, but came away from the reunion with the idea that her birth father had died.

Says Jensen: "I had thought for years about finding the kids but there were a number of reasons why I didn't. I was concerned that the children may not know they were adopted. I didn't want to just drop in on their lives like a bombshell."

Father and daughter talked awhile and exchanged addresses and phone numbers. Jensen went home, told his wife the news, and realized he had not asked Allison if she had any children. He called and found he was grandfather to three.

Lois Rosencutter and George Jensen married when they

were seventeen and had George junior right away. Both struggled to make ends meet but there wasn't enough money. Four years later, when George and Lois divorced, it was clear the children, then aged two and four, would have much better lives if they were adopted by a family who wanted and could afford them. The lawyer handling the divorce knew of a family looking to adopt and the procedure was quickly arranged. Jensen had had the tattoos put on his chest when George junior and Edie Jo were born so their names would always be close to his heart.

"I'm not a religious person but there has to be somebody, somewhere that steered us together," Jensen says. "It's just too much to write off to coincidence."

Says Allison: "I think it was meant to be; it was meant for us to come full circle and to be part of each other's lives again. There MUST be a higher being that has pushed us together."

Jensen, who is now retired from a shipyard, lives with his third wife and sees Allison and his grandchildren as often as possible. George junior was also reunited with his father.

"They fill a big hole in my life," says Jensen.

As Barbara Deck leaned over the sink in a public restroom, she heard the infuriated snorting. She turned to face an enraged, twelve-hundred-pound Brahma bull, ready to charge.

Barbara grew up on ranches in North Dakota and had been around livestock since she was a child. She also loved going to the rodeo, with the exception of one event. She had once seen a bull break both legs of a rider and didn't care to watch the bull-riding events anymore. When it came time for them, Barbara would simply excuse herself and come back later for the rest of the show.

While watching a rodeo in Minot, South Dakota, Barbara noticed the bull riding event approaching. She left her seat and went to the arena's ladies' room, which was located down a long hallway near the entrance.

While Barbara was on her way to the ladies' room, bedlam

was breaking loose in the ring. A bull threw its rider and chased a rodeo clown out of the arena. The animal then jumped three separate five-and-one-half-foot restraining fences and made its way to the interior of the building. It ran down the hallway before bursting into the rest room where Barbara stood washing her hands.

"I heard the loudspeaker announce that a bull had jumped a fence but I really didn't give it much thought," Barbara says. "The thought in my mind was, 'Well, I'll just go on washing my hands, I'm safe here.' After all, you have to go down a long, narrow hallway to enter the rest room. I know for a fact that big ranch animals don't like that type of confinement."

Nonetheless, not three feet away stood an enormous, snorting, adrenaline-charged bull, very annoyed with the day's torment.

"The first thing I noticed was the bull had one of his rear legs poised in the air," Barbara says. "That's the posture a bull assumes just before he charges."

Barbara had her back to the sink as the bull lowered his head and rushed in like a runaway locomotive. There wasn't room for the animal to turn and gore her with his horns, but he did pin her against the wall with his head. At one point, she grabbed a horn to keep her body from impalement. A split second later, the bull whirled and destroyed the sink with a single kick of his hind leg. Barbara grabbed what was left of the sink fixture and kept it between her and the bull. Water was now shooting from the wall and that seemed to distract the animal. Glancing to her left, above the stall doors, Barbara saw a row of heads, watching the rampaging bull with wide eyes. After what seemed like an eternity, several cowboys came into the rest room, told the women in the stalls to stay put, and pulled Barbara into the hall, all while distracting the Brahma.

Barbara was hospitalized for injuries to her shoulder and arm and was later compensated by the rodeo group. A judge ruled that, while the bull performed a routine even an Olympic steeplechase horse would have trouble duplicating, the restraining fences should have been higher.

State District Judge Lupe Salinas didn't quite know how or from where he knew the shopper who had just nodded hello. The man pushing the shopping cart through the poultry section admitted he, too, was at a loss for a connection.

Then a name popped into the mind of Judge Salinas.

"Samuel Ettipio?"

The shopper returned a long, puzzled expression that indicated the name was correct.

"Samuel Joseph Ettipio?" Judge Salinas said, somewhat more forcefully as an image formed in his mind.

"Yes, that's right, I'm Samuel Ettipio. But I still don't know where I know you from."

"I was the judge on your case."

"Oh, shit. . . ." Ettipio said.

In June, four months before, Judge Salinas had sentenced Ettipio to twenty-two years in prison for selling cocaine. Normal procedure called for Ettipio to be taken from the courtroom to prison that same day. But, here, on the following Halloween night, was Ettipio, casually shopping for poultry in a large supermarket in Houston, Texas, seemingly without a care in the world.

Ettipio quickly blurted he didn't really know the law, but that he had been released by the sheriffs on the day of sentencing. He said that he had quit doing or selling drugs, that he had a regular income from a legitimate business, and that he had really been getting his life together.

"I was at a complete loss to explain how or why this man was back out on the streets," Judge Salinas said. "I said I didn't know the law either if this guy was out free. My first thought was there could be some corruption in the court system and that he had paid somebody for his freedom. So I told Ettipio to say nothing more until he could consult with his lawyer; that I would be calling all the parties in the case back together in court first thing in the morning."

Judge Salinas wondered if he should take the man into custody right then and there, but decided against it. "I was on personal time and I'm not in the enforcement end of the law business," said Salinas.

The next day, the judge called an emergency session with Ettipio, his attorney, the prosecuting attorney, and the sheriff who was responsible for processing Ettipio into jail.

"I found the clerk of my court had made a mistake on a computer," Judge Salinas said. "The sheriff's deputy brought to court the paperwork he had received on the case. On the form was printed code "28," which means: "Not guilty, release the offender." However, the clerk should have entered "38," code for "Time in prison plus a fine." There was no double check procedure, so Ettipio was released entirely by mistake."

Ettipio was returned to jail after the emergency session, although his conviction was being appealed.

But he might have remained a free man had he not made that fateful decision to go grocery shopping.

Sergeant Virgin King, of the Santa Clara County Jail in California, booked a suspect, Robert Magoon, for allegedly violating his parole from the California Youth Authority. In another part of the facility, another inmate, Michael Robert Magoon, was being held on robbery charges. Sergeant King kept looking at the two names.

"When Robert Magoon came in, we asked him if he had any relatives in the area," said King, who is now a lieutenant. "Robert said he didn't know of any. He had mostly grown up in foster homes. And then we specifically asked, 'Would your father be here?' "

Robert said he had not seen his father since he was a very small child. He wasn't even sure what his dad looked like. But the deputies could see both Magoons had red hair and sported tattoos in about the same places. So the lawmen followed up on their hunch.

"We went back to the cell of Michael Robert Magoon and asked him if he had a son in the area," Lieutenant King says. "Michael Robert told us that he had a son, Robert, eighteen or nineteen years ago, but that his ex-wife had taken the boy and left town. Although he had searched for him from time to time, he said he never saw either of them again."

Robert Magoon was separated from his father shortly after birth. He spent most of his youth in foster homes and ran away from the last one when he was fourteen. Periodically, he had searched for his dad, looking in files like the records of the Department of Motor Vehicles. But nobody seemed to have any information.

A deputy asked for the name of Magoon's ex-wife and returned to Robert Magoon's cell and asked for his mother's name. That named checked out so the deputies cross-checked young Magoon's date of birth. Michael knew it immediately so the deputies broke the happy tidings and asked Robert if he wanted to write a letter to his father, requesting a visitation.

"Normally, we don't allow family visits, but since it had been so many years since they had seen each other, I decided it would be O.K. in this case," Lieutenant King said.

Both Magoons were nervous and excited before the meeting. At first they shook hands, then they hugged and sat down to talk.

"It was almost instant recognition when they saw each other," King said. "And as they talked, they found they shared a lot of common interests. Robert has an older brother who called and wanted to come in and meet his father. The brother also had not seen the father since he was a toddler."

Said the proud dad of Robert: "He's so handsome. Tears come to my eyes when I see my boy."

Michael Magoon said he had no idea the boy was being raised in foster homes. He also had some fatherly advice for his son: he wanted Robert to keep his nose clean and to learn auto painting, the trade the older Magoon had plied for years, when he got out of jail.

When Linda Porter, of Big Bear Lake, California, was applying for her passport, she received her original birth certificate. She knew she was adopted but had never known her birth name. There, on her birth record, she saw for the first time the name of her biological father: Edward Gallagher.

A year later, Linda was reading her town's weekly newspaper, *The Grizzly*. In a news column about local people, the paper mentioned that an Ed Gallagher and his wife were back from a short trip to Arizona.

"I'm usually so busy at work, I hardly ever pick up the paper, but the first thought in my mind was that this person could be a son or cousin or some other relation to my father," Linda says. "My mother had always said my birth father didn't want to have anything to do with me."

Linda made a mental note to check out the local Gallagher as soon as she got a chance. But summer slid into the next year's spring before she thought again of making the call. Big Bear Lake is a small ski and fishing resort of about fifteen thousand permanent residents in the San Bernardino Mountains, three hours east of Los Angeles.

When Linda had gotten married at eighteen, her mother told her the man who raised her was not her biological father. She explained how the first marriage was a hasty wartime union on the East Coast and that the family split up when Linda was only three months old. Later, Linda's mother remarried in California.

For years, Linda made and sold very popular ceramic masks of faces. She had become intrigued with faces because she had a recurring dream wherein she was a little girl sitting in a large, sunny kitchen with a man who was washing the breakfast dishes.

But in the dream she could not clearly see the man's face.

The dream was always the same. She would ask the man a question and get a brief glimpse of his face as he quickly turned to answer. She asked her mother if the dream could be from her childhood, but Linda's mother could not explain the dream either. Both women were especially at a loss to explain why the dream had recurred for thirty-seven years.

Finally, Linda got around to calling the Gallagher listed in Big Bear's eighty-three-page telephone book. Linda explained to the person who answered that she was doing genealogy research. Birth dates, names, and other information from Linda's birth certificate matched, but Ed Gallagher was away just then, traveling. Linda didn't know it at the time but the person to whom she was speaking was Ed Gallagher's son and her half-brother. Linda left her name and number with the Gallaghers and said she would call back.

"It's a one-in-a-million shot that this person is my father," Linda told her husband, Terry. The next time she decided to call Gallagher, she lost her nerve and asked Terry to make the call for her. Even as Terry dialed the number, he felt there was simply no way this Gallagher could be Linda's dad.

This time, Ed Gallagher was at home. He confirmed who he was and asked Terry when he could see Linda.

Stunned, Terry hung up the phone and told Linda it was true. It was her father.

"I was a little hesitant about the reunion because I had always assumed from my mother that he didn't want anything to do with me," Linda said. "So I thought it would be 'hello, nice to meet you, goodbye.' Right off the bat, I told him I realized this was a one-time thing and I would be out of his hair in minutes."

But within several minutes of the reunion, Linda learned that coincidence had stacked atop coincidence. Father and daughter lived only several minutes away from each other. Both had unknowingly moved to the small resort town at the same time twelve years ago. When the Porters first moved to Big Bear Lake, Linda lived only two blocks from her father and had taken many evening strolls down his street and past his house. Linda also discovered she was related to people—through Gallagher—with whom she had been socializing for years in Big Bear Lake.

Linda has also visited friends many times at the houses behind and right next to Gallagher's current home. "I explained my recurring dream to my dad and he confirmed every detail in it," Linda says. "It was his face that I had been seeing in the dream all those years."

"I also found out that I was three years old, not three months, when my mother left for California, and that my dad wrote and sent money for a long while. At the time, he was tied up with a government job on the East Coast and couldn't just pack up and move."

When Ed Gallagher arrived in California to pick Linda up for her fourth birthday, he found an empty house.

"Somebody told him that my mother and I had moved to Alaska," Linda says. "After that, he spent seven years searching for us in Alaska.

"As time went on, I ran into more people here in town who knew us both. I found out I have four half-brothers and we're all getting acquainted. For instance, we went to Europe together last year and we now spend holidays together.

"My mother still doesn't know I found my dad and I really don't know how she will handle it when she finds out. But I think there's a higher power at work here, something we just don't understand at all," Linda says. "It's all just too, too much for a coincidence."

Judy Musso liked the sound of William Vogue's voice. He was the guy a local dating service had referred to her. So, after talking to him for an hour on the phone, she agreed to go out on a date.

When William arrived, Judy squinted hard in the porch light to more clearly see his features. Then she gasped:

"Ray? Ray Voge?"

Her date, William, was Ray, the man she had fallen madly in love with thirty-two years earlier on a warm San Diego beach. William stood frozen in place on the sidewalk looking up at Judy on the porch.

"Judy? Judy Hotchkiss?"

Vogue recognized Judy at the same instant. "My heart almost stopped when I saw her," Vogue says. "And then we stood on the porch, holding hands and gazing into each other's eyes for fifteen minutes."

Six hours later, William Vogue and Judy Musso picked up where they left off thirty-two years ago and decided to get married.

When Judy was eighteen, in May of 1957, she first met Vogue, who then went by the name of Ray Wilhelm Voge. Voge was staying at the Balboa Hotel in San Diego on vacation and went to hear a Tommy Dorsey concert. He saw a stunning, classy young woman and asked her to dance. Ray and Judy never missed another dance and spent the rest of the evening together. They also took a late walk in the moonlight on the beach.

"I'll never forget it," Ray says. "She had on a light blue formal gown overlaid with lace. And she was wearing a tiara."

Although Ray was thirty and Judy only eighteen, they met for breakfast the next day and spent that entire day together. They had in mind spending many days together.

But Musso's father didn't approve of the budding romance because of the age difference. After meeting secretly for nine months, Voge, a ship mechanic, was transferred away from California and lost contact. Voge called at the Hotchkiss home a couple of years later but her father said Judy had been married. Voge later changed his name because Voge and Wilhelm were too often mispronounced.

"It was love at first sight, we were both young and we just fell instantly head over heels in love," Vogue says.

After that date with fate in Houston, Judy and Ray got married three months later. The years between must have been pretty hard on Vogue. Although it was Judy's second marriage, it was the twenty-first for Vogue.

Peggy Atwood of Altus, Oklahoma, enjoys watching the NBC show *Unsolved Mysteries*, but is usually too busy taking care of the children enrolled in the day-care center she operates from her home. However, on July 4, there were no kids to watch, so Peggy made a cup of coffee and sat down in the living room. She was happy to be able to watch the whole show, which that evening was the third anniversary special.

Halfway through the program, Peggy's eyes almost popped out of her head. In a segment about the capture of a convicted murderer, a witness in Arizona was interviewed. Lavar Bates's name flashed on the screen as he told the camera what he had seen.

Peggy immediately lost interest in the show. Lavar Bates was her former boyfriend and father to her daughter, Kimber. Bates never knew he had fathered a daughter by Peggy, who had been looking for him for the last thirty-one years.

In 1958, Lavar and Peggy were planning on getting married. Because they lived sixty miles apart, they usually visited each other on weekends. But when the eighteen-year-old Peggy came to visit Lavar and found a picture of another woman on his mirror, she stormed out and drove back home. The next day, Lavar was transferred out of state by his company without learning Peggy was expecting his child. After this, Peggy had married and had three other children who all knew their father. But Kimber grew up wondering who her dad was, if he was alive, where he was from, if he was healthy, and a thousand other questions.

"Right after I saw Lavar's name on TV, I immediately grabbed the phone and called my other daughter in California," Peggy says. "She could barely understand me, I was so excited. I didn't know if I was dreaming or imagining it all or what, so I asked her to tape the program since it airs two hours later there."

Through a series of calls, Peggy reached the production offices of *Unsolved Mysteries*. She explained who she was and that Bates had a daughter who was most anxious to meet him. The show said they would contact Bates and let him know.

"The next Sunday, I heard his voice for the first time in thirty-one years," Peggy says. "He said, 'This is Lavar, Peggy. I understand we have a daughter.' Just thinking about it gives me cold chills because I had missed the segment with Lavar on it three times before. The only reason I saw it was because there were no kids to cook for that evening."

The next call Peggy made was to Kimber. She told her daughter that her father had been located and that he would love to see the daughter he hadn't even known about. Kimber was speechless. "And when I told her I had located her father while watching a TV program, she just couldn't believe it," Peggy said. "Kimber and I both think it was just God's will."

Lavar Bates now calls Kimber frequently, sends his grand-children gifts, and otherwise takes part in Kimber's life. He checks in with Peggy periodically.

"It's just wonderful," says Peggy. "We're not romantic or anything; it's just like an old friend calling. It's been thirty-one years, but now that we all know each other again, it seems like he's always been here."

Don Martin lost touch with La Donna, his firstborn daughter, thirty-two years ago after a nasty divorce. Martin's only clue to the whereabouts of La Donna was a letter written by his ex-wife in 1963. The letter mostly asked Martin not to meddle in her new marriage and mentioned that her last name had become Splane, that they were an Air Force family who moved a lot and that, in addition to La Donna, they had a son named John and a daughter named Karen.

Although Don Martin had ten other children, he always wondered about La Donna. So when he traveled, he always picked up the phone book and looked for a John Splane. Although he had been to several dozen different cities, he had never had any luck.

Then, around his fifty-second birthday, Don Martin started having dreams about La Donna. The dreams were probably triggered when Martin's mother gave him a box of old pictures and copies of La Donna's birth announcement.

He also came across the letter from 1963 among his keep-sakes. On a whim, Don picked up the Dallas phone book and, as he had done so many times before, turned the pages to see if a John Splane was listed. There was a man by that name living in Mesquite, Texas, a town only a few miles from Martin's house in Balch Springs. Don dialed the number three or four times but nobody ever answered. Martin had almost given up when, one morning, he thought he would try the number early, about 7 A.M.

"Hello, I'm trying to locate a John Splane who has a sister named La Donna and a sister named Karen."

The voice replied: "Well, my name is John Splane and I do have sisters named Karen and La Donna."

Don felt as if he was going to pass out, so he plopped down in a chair and said: "You just don't know how long I've searched for you. I am La Donna's father."

John said, "Are you really Mr. Martin? Why, I know all about you." He explained that La Donna had been living only two miles from Don's house for the last twenty years. However, La Donna and her family had just moved into a new house and John did not yet have her phone number. John offered to put Don in touch with his ex-wife, to whom he had not spoken in over three decades. Martin took a deep breath, fixed a cup of coffee, and let ten minutes pass to settle his nerves. He then called La Donna's mother who said she would pass Don's number on to La Donna.

La Donna had searched for her father off and on over the years as the family changed bases and thought she might go the rest of her life without seeing him.

"It had been so long, I wouldn't even allow myself to dream about meeting my father," La Donna says. "It was the last thing on my mind.

"When my mother told me dad had turned up and I was supposed to call him, I thought she was kidding," says La Donna. "It took a full two minutes for her to convince me she was serious."

La Donna called and the two arranged to have lunch. At first, she thought she would be calling an old man whose last wish was to see his daughter. "On the way to lunch, I thought, 'What am I going to talk about? What am I going to say?'" La Donna says. "I was shaking so badly with nerves, I almost couldn't drive."

But within half an hour, they discovered that La Donna had been visiting a friend who lived right next door to the Martins. Moreover, the church La Donna attended was just down the block from her father's house. She was pleased to see that her father looks fifteen years younger than his actual age and that they share interests in football and writing poetry. Martin also wanted to start getting acquainted with his three grandchildren.

Their next date was the Texas State Fair several weeks later. "Just pretend you're twelve and I'm thirty," Don said to La Donna. "We've got a lot of catching up to do."

Don works nights and frequently sleeps days, including Sundays. But whenever he can arrange it, he and La Donna go to the Hickory Tree Baptist Church, just a block distant from the Martin home.

"I believe in miracles now," Don Martin says.

While standing in a line for lottery tickets in a store in Oceanside, California, Marcella Baxter heard two men talking about her home town in Minneapolis. One of the men mentioned the Dunwoody Institute and that caught Marcella's ear.

"Is Dunwoody still there?" Marcella asked, turning around.

One of the men, George Sanborn, doesn't ordinarily buy

lottery tickets but he was picking up a few for his son who lives in Minneapolis. Talk turned to the old Minnesota stamping grounds, and Sanborn soon asked Marcella if she, by any chance, knew a man by the name of "Cork" Anderson.

"Well, you could say that," Marcella said calmly, "I was married to him and he is the father of my children."

Then Marcella looked harder at Sanborn, thinking he looked familiar. So she asked if, by any chance, his name was George Sanborn. It was.

Sanborn and Marcella's first husband had worked together as security guards for the Du Pont Company in Richfield, Minnesota, during World War II.

Says Marcella, who is now widowed from her second husband: "I hadn't seen George in thirty-seven years and now he lives fifteen minutes away from me in California. Back in Minnesota, my first husband and I and George and his current wife used to go out all the time. None of us won with the lottery tickets we bought that day, but it was sure great being reacquainted with old friends."

Tammy Harris, twenty-two, of Roanoke, Virginia, had been searching for her birth mother for five years. Six months earlier, Tammy and another woman, Joyce Schultz, had been hired at a busy convenience store on the same day. Tammy could never have guessed that her new coworker was her natural mother. Tammy worked an earlier shift so she and Joyce did not get a chance to talk or be around each other very much. Even more surprising than the coincidence of their working at the same store, Tammy's birth mother lived two blocks from her own house.

When Tammy was sixteen, she had become intensely curious about her birth parents. She only knew that when they were very young, she and her brothers had been taken away from their parents by the county because her father was in jail and her mother had a problem with alcohol abuse. Eventually, Tammy was adopted at two and a half. Her two brothers were adopted by separate families. When she was eighteen, she gave birth to her own daughter, Maria. The experience further spurred Tammy's desire to find her mother.

"Because I spent so much time talking about my baby, the question always came up of how old was I when I took my first steps," Tammy says, "or how old was I when I first sat up. Well, I had no way of knowing. There was just a big blank spot in my life."

Tammy went to her social worker on the day before her twenty-first birthday, found the name of her birth mother, Joyce Schultz, and the town where she first lived, and started her search. She looked in old phone books, high school year books, through marriage licenses and property records, always looking for a woman whose name was spelled "Shultz." But she didn't have any luck, even after taking out a newspaper ad announcing she was looking for her birth mother.

One day, a coworker asked Tammy if she was having any luck in her search.

"Luck with what?" asked Joyce as she walked in to work and overheard the question. Tammy then explained the circumstances of her infancy. It was the first Joyce knew of Tammy's adoption in early life.

"Well, do you know if you have a birth certificate?" Joyce asked.

"Sure, just let me dig it out of my purse," said Tammy, who always kept the document with her.

Joyce read the birth certificate and knew then she was looking at her daughter, taken from her so long ago. But she played her cards close to her chest and showed no emotion. Joyce asked only if Tammy had any baby pictures of herself.

"I have one and one only," Tammy said.

"Well, why don't you lend it to me," said Joyce. "I might know somebody who knows something about where your parents are. That last name sounds real familiar."

Tammy recalled: "I went home, got the picture, and left it

at the store that day. After all the searching and digging I had done, my strongest lead was that this woman might know where my parents were. And off and on, the thought popped into my mind that maybe Joyce could be my mother. After three days, I was a nervous wreck."

Eventually, the store manager, Ron Lynch, suggested that Tammy ask Joyce directly if she was her mother. He thought Tammy was losing too much sleep over the whole affair.

"I can't do that," Tammy said. "What if she *is* my real mother and she doesn't want to tell me?"

As soon as those words were out of Tammy's mouth, Joyce walked into Ron's office and asked if she could speak to him alone. Tammy went outside, waiting and pacing. She was called back fifteen minutes later.

The first thing Tammy saw were two pictures lying on Ron's desk. One picture was the one Tammy had lent Joyce. The other, which Joyce had brought in, was a picture of a man holding an infant. The little girl smiling into the camera was the same in both shots.

Tammy looked at the pictures, looked up at Ron, then at Joyce and back at the pictures. Ron broke the awkward silence.

"You know what I'm going to tell you, don't you?" Ron looked at Tammy for several seconds and said: "Your search is over, Tammy."

"It still didn't click in," Tammy says. "I didn't know if Joyce had *FOUND* my mother or *WAS* my mother. So I turned and asked her if she was my mom. She said yes, and I just fell apart, shaking uncontrollably and crying."

Mother and daughter fell into each other's arms. Joyce sobbed, over and over, "My baby! My baby!"

"I didn't really need to know anything about why I was taken away," Tammy says. "All I wanted to know was that my mother did want me, that she was alive and OK, and that she loved me. That's all I needed."

Tammy later learned that Joyce said nothing when she first

looked at the birth certificate because she wasn't sure how Tammy felt about her birth parents. Joyce knew that Tammy had been confiding in Ron about it all so she, Joyce, asked Ron if Tammy would reject or embrace her natural mother.

Joyce soon put Tammy in touch with her birth father, who is putting together a family reunion that will include 250 people related to Tammy by birth and by adoption.

"We've got a lot of catching up to do," Tammy says. "There are many, many uncles, aunts, cousins, and other relatives I'm going to meet for the first time."

Joyce and Tammy now want to search for Tammy's brothers, Terry and Tim, who would now be twenty-one and twenty-five.

10
HIGH-VOLTAGE, VANGUARD VACATIONS

When Sir Friedrich von Kahlbutz, a powerful knight who lived from 1651 to 1702 in Neustadt, Germany, made his now-famous boast, he never thought it would come true.

According to legend, the knight killed a shepherd who refused to submit to a local custom—letting the nobleman ravish his bride on the pair's wedding night.

"If I am responsible for the shepherd's death, let my body never decay," Kahlbutz is said to have declared in his defense.

Almost three hundred years later, Kahlbutz's undecomposed body is still being viewed by tourists. The body has been studied, measured, and weighed, but scientists can't say for sure why Kahlbutz's corpse never turned to dust. It rests today in a stone church in a glass-topped coffin rigged with burglar alarms. The corpse weighs only about twenty pounds and the skin is leathery, but it lies intact surrounded by Kahlbutz's helmet, breastplate, lance, and other trappings of office. According to one caretaker, the knight's fingernails must be clipped weekly. Kahlbutz fathered eleven children borne by his wife and perhaps thirty more borne by peasant women in his domain. But nothing done during Kahlbutz's life went over as well as his death. One Neustadt official reckons one hundred thousand people yearly come to see the mummy, making it the area's largest and most profitable tourist attraction. The knight is gaining wider attention because Neustadt, a city in the former nation of East Germany, is now more accessible to tourists.

Boise City, Oklahoma, shares something in common with most large cities in Germany. They were all bombed during World War II by at least one B-17 Flying Fortress.

In the wee hours of July 5, 1943, a B-17 from Dalhart Army Air Force Base in Texas mistook the lights surrounding the Boise City town square for a practice range. Circling several times on bombing runs, six practice bombs containing only four pounds of explosive each were dropped, striking a garage, the Baptist church, near a boardinghouse, and a sidewalk. Two bombs struck only ground and several were duds. Nobody was hurt but one bomb did come close to striking a parked fuel truck. The raid ended when somebody turned off the power, throwing the whole town into darkness.

At Dalhart, the base commander, Major C. E. Lancaster, concluded after an investigation: "The bombing was a mistake in navigation." The real practice-bombing range was near Conlen, Texas, about forty-five miles south of Boise City. Today, the bomb casings from the infamous raid draw tourists to several displays in a local law office, a hardware store, and in the offices of the chamber of commerce.

The area was unwittingly bombed again in March, 1945, when two Army Air Force bombers dropped several bombs on a field outside Boise City, creating a grass fire and leaving several craters.

The Boise City bombing will be marked by a special fifty-year anniversary observation in July, 1993.

For those who never really grew up and still harbor a juvenile desire deep down inside to play first base (or any base) for the Dodgers, or drive an Indianapolis race car, or be a jazz star, they can indulge themselves, thanks to fantasy vacations.

The L.A. Dodgers offer what they claim is an unforgettable week of baseball at Dodgertown in Vero Beach, Florida. Sixty-two ordinary guys become Dodgers for a week during the off season when they are instructed by former Dodgers like Duke Snider, Reggie Smith, and others. Tom Lasorda puts in a one-day appearance. (The team began in 1890, when it was known as the "Trolley Dodgers" because there were many tracks and street cars you had to evade in the streets of Brooklyn, New York, their original home.) Instruction, meals, and lodging are identical to what paid-to-play Dodgers experience in spring training. The fantasy players, however, have several hours of free time daily during which they can fish, lounge in or near an Olympic-size pool, or play tennis, golf, basketball, cards, or billiards. World Series films are shown nightly. You must bring your own glove, spikes, personal clothes, and chewing tobacco. The week in baseball heaven ends with a game between instructors and students, who must be at least thirty and in good health. Typical attendees include attorneys, judges, musicians, accountants, geologists, and many others. One baseball camper came back with his seventy-one-year-old father, a real estate developer. Fees range from $4000 to $4500.

Sports World of San Francisco offers similar camps with the Oakland As, Minnesota Twins, Cleveland Indians, and San Francisco Giants. Sports World also has off-season, four-day basketball camps with players from the Lakers and the Warriors doing the coaching chores. Fees here are as tall as an NBA center, ranging from $2,995 to $3,995.

The Skip Barber Racing School in Canaan, Connecticut, offers a ninety-minute "Intro" course in racing in a genuine Mondiale B-1 Formula Ford. Twenty-one other race tracks around the nation offer instruction on race-style downshifting, braking, and cornering, and allow amateur drivers to experience the thrill of speeding around a genuine track and seeing the checkered flag waved at the finish line. And the Jim Russell Street Survival Program in Salinas, California, puts pupils in a Mitsubishi Galant at the Laguna Seca Raceway in Monterey and teaches them how to be better drivers by avoiding traffic accidents altogether. Instruction includes a class that allows laymen to drive a fire-breathing B-1 Formula Ford race car for two hours on the track.

Perhaps the ultimate vicarious pleasure for amateur jazz musicians is a ticket to the Skidmore Jazz Institute at Skidmore College in Saratoga Springs, New York. The institute offers a two-week camp every June wherein attendees can jam with the likes of Buddy Baker, Mil Hinton, and other jazz greats. Jazz campers should have at least a high-school-level playing ability and range in age from fifteen to mid-fifties. The camp ends with the guest musicians playing sets on stage for audiences at Skidmore. But the biggest treat is when the campers attend, and play a set at, the Newport Jazz Festival.

Top Gun Aviation of Fullerton, California, straps would-be fighter pilots into a plane that resembles a jet fighter and takes them aloft—with a real pilot—looking for bogeys to shoot down. Instead of guns or rockets, opponents fire microwaves at each other. When a well-aimed blast of microwave fire hits a similarly modified plane, the plane spews white smoke and plummets toward the earth.

For those into male bonding, the Real Man's Mid-Life Crisis Tour, in San Diego, offers a fifteen-day guided tour through Thailand. The tour is heavy on typical vacation treats like sampling the local cuisine, shopping for exotic items, and sportfishing. At the start, there's a quick visit to Bangkok's Kangaroo Bar, renowned as one of the world's five sleaziest bars. The trip is studded with excursions to macho attractions like the Bridge on the River Kwai, a structure for which eight thousand prisoners died while building it in World War II, and a glimpse at the infamous Golden Triangle, the source of much of the world's illicit drugs. The male tourists also: go to a Thai boxing match where the slugging takes place with feet and hands; ride on an elephant safari; visit the fifteen-ton, solid gold Golden Buddha that marks the resting place of Buddha; and visit other meaningful cultural attractions like massage parlors, nude beaches, back-alley fleshpots, and the world's sixth and seventh most sleazy bars. Cost for the two-week getaway: thirty-five hundred dollars.

Of course, not all theme vacations are designed for men. Mothers' Camp at Big Bear Lake, California, offers a Friday-to-Sunday night retreat for harried moms who can get a massage, sip champagne, float around on an alpine lake, ride horses, hike, ski in the winter, or do anything except pick up after husbands and children, both of whom must remain at home.

Merry Widow Cruises of Tampa, Florida, are dance cruises for single, widowed, or divorced women of ages thirty to ninety who like to dance. Back in 1977, organizer Phyllis Zeno noticed her seven-day cruises had a preponderance of women but no men to dance with them. Phyllis had discovered a need and filled it by rounding up men who were graduates of Fred Astaire and Arthur Murray dance studios. She offered them a free cruise in exchange for being a gentleman host every evening. Hosts change dinner tables every evening, so every woman aboard gets a chance to know and dance with each host. Gentleman hosts are not allowed to take tips or gifts or show partiality to any one woman. For every twenty to forty women on a cruise, there are four to eight gentlemen hosts. Ms. Zeno organizes four or five trips a year through the AAA Auto Club South in Tampa.

While there are dude ranches galore, one outfit recreates the conditions of an actual cattle drive as it used to be in 1870. The MW Ranch near Hudson, Colorado, takes on twenty-eight cow-boys and cowgirls (40 percent of MW "drovers" are women) per drive and, four times yearly, drives a herd of longhorns and mixed breeds sixty-five miles. Driving cattle is a slow process, so it takes six and a half days to move the herd sixty-five miles down one of three Old West–style trails.

"Of course, modern cowboys are faced with a few obstacles and problems they didn't have back in the old days," says Bill Diekroeger, MW Ranch trail boss. "Cowboys in 1870 didn't have to get permission from the Forest Service."

À la Billy Crystal's gang in the movie *City Slickers*, the campers must saddle and care for their horses, take turns at rustling up the 1870-style grub (flapjacks, buffalo roast, son-of-a-gun stew, soppy and spuds, molasses custard, spotted pup pudding, and boiled coffee) and watching over the herd at night ("nighthawking") on two-hour shifts. At trail's end, there's a contest for those who toted along shootin' irons, a range rodeo, and a fandango, "stompin' " to live cowboy music. And in keeping with the time period, "likker" is consumed from the company supply in a tin cup.

Another tourist attraction that evoked the old West was discovered to have a longer history than anybody ever intended. In 1911, a small-potatoes train robber, Elmer McCurdy, while waiting for a train that carried money for an Indian reservation, held up the wrong train, shot a man, and stole forty-six dollars and two gallons of whiskey. A sheriff's posse caught up with McCurdy when he stopped for the night and was sleeping off the effects of too much of his ill-gotten gains. The sheriff testified in court that McCurdy went for his six-shooter, as best as he could under the circumstances, but the posse gunned the robber down first and brought him back to town slung over a saddle. Elmer had no kin thereabouts so a local mortician volunteered to prepare the body and take care of burial.

The next major news about Elmer broke in 1975 at the Nu-Pike Amusement Park in Long Beach, California. Shown as a wax dummy, McCurdy had been performing for the public by hanging from a noose until a TV worker accidentally knocked off his arm, saw bones, and found the dummy was actually a human body. Los Angeles Coroner Thomas Naguchi (the "coroner to the stars") worked for three years on the case to trace McCurdy's roots. He found that back in 1911, the mortician mummified McCurdy's corpse after reading about techniques used in ancient Egypt. But the mortician used over three hundred times the necessary amount of arsenic, getting Elmer into a far more thoroughly pickled state in death than the robber could ever attain on his own with cheap whiskey while alive. For a while, the mortician exhibited McCurdy at a funeral home for five cents a peek, and then sold his body to people who displayed it in traveling circus sideshows and Wild West shows. After the accident in Long Beach, Naguchi eventually pieced together McCurdy's history. His remains were shipped to a boot hill cemetery in Guthrie, Oklahoma, for a long overdue burial. Naguchi also discovered from the trajectory of the fatal bullets that Elmer was shot while sleeping. But there was no peace for McCurdy, who continued making the news.

Becky Luker, owner of three Stone Lion Inns in Guthrie, Oklahoma, wrote a series of twelve murder mysteries that are played out by guests on Friday and Saturday evenings during the summer. One of the mysteries is based on the life and death of Elmer McCurdy and requires a trip to his grave in search of clues. Because the people attending the mysteries are all dressed in period costumes, some locals jumped to conclusions and mistook the mystery play for devil worshipping. Dozens of newspaper articles eventually appeared about the train robber being the center of Satanic worship. Mrs. Luker quelled the reports by agreeing to make the stop at Elmer's grave only during daylight hours and to act quietly and reverently, something McCurdy had never before experienced.

A tourist destination in Eastland, Texas, also features an embalmed body—but of a horned toad. In 1897, a Bible, newspapers, and the usual mementos were placed in the cornerstone of Eastland's courthouse along with one last-minute addition: a horned toad, one of those spiked lizards that fits in the palm of your hand. In 1928, thirty-one years later, the courthouse was demolished to make room for a larger structure and the cornerstone was opened. Judge Ed S. Pritchard removed the Bible and newspaper and noticed the dust-covered toad. It was fished out by a local oil man who then handed it to the Reverend Frank S. Singleton, pastor of the First Methodist Church. The pastor held up the toad for the three thousand bystanders to see. Suddenly, it twitched—the toad was still alive—and probably blinked like a fast Morse code signal in the harsh Texas sunshine. The townspeople consulted a herpetologist who said it would indeed be possible for a horned toad to live that long if ants, the toad's favorite meal, had found their way into the cornerstone. Moreover, the creature is cold-blooded and can drastically slow its metabolism. The toad was promptly dubbed Old Rip, in remembrance of Rip Van Winkle. Rip then made headlines nationwide and was taken to Washington, D.C., and shown to then-president Calvin Coolidge. Unfortunately, the air outside the limestone cornerstone was too damp, causing Old Rip to expire from pneumonia in January, 1929, only eleven months after his liberation. But he wasn't forgotten. The townsfolk embalmed Old Rip in 1929 and put him on display in a tiny casket lined with velvet and satin. Old Rip again made headlines in 1962 when John Connally made a campaign whistle-stop in Eastland while running for governor. But Connally thought the toad was being presented to him so he picked up the preserved Rip by a rear leg and broke it off. Since 1962, Eastland has insured that Rip lies in true peace by covering his coffin with glass and has further immortalized his memory with an annual parade. If you're in town, there are special tie tacks, post cards, belt buckles, bolo ties, and T-shirts with Rip's pre-and-postmortem likeness available. Today, his body lies inside the town courthouse.

The Hollywood Death Site Tour takes you—via a hearse with "kick-the-bucket seats"—to the sites where celebrities Sal Mineo, Jack Webb, John Belushi, and seventy-three other stars met their ends, sort of a Death Styles of the Rich and Famous, if you will. Operated by a firm known as Grave Line Tours, the tour visits the chintzy motel where Janice Joplin died of a drug overdose, past the spot where William Frawley (Fred Mertz on *I Love Lucy*), hit the sidewalk on Hollywood Boulevard after a fatal heart attack, the apartment building where Jack Cassidy died in a fire, and past the rented mansion where Sharon Tate was killed by the Manson clan. You'll see the home where Jean Harlow died in 1926, the place where Bugsy Siegel suffered a hit by the mob, and the house in which Lana Turner's fourteen-year-old daughter, Cheryl, stabbed Lana's hoodlum boyfriend, Johnny Stompanato, with a kitchen knife. The tour lasts two hours and visits other sites like the road where Montgomery Clift crashed his car into a telephone pole. The tour does not visit Marilyn Monroe's death house but does drive by the pharmacy where she filled the fatal prescription. However, the tour is not entirely filled with sickness, drug overdoses, accidents, and murder. The final stop is the house where the original Rin Tin Tin died peacefully of old age.

Tinseltown also features the Hollywood Walk of Fame, which has some nineteen hundred stars embedded in the sidewalks of Hollywood and Vine boulevards. Included among the stars of recent fame like Bob Hope and Marilyn Monroe are big names that haven't been in the news lately. Lalo Schifrin, Cubby Broccoli, the Reverend James Cleveland, Tich Wilkerson-Kassel, Ernst Schoedsach, Alla Nazimova, King Baggot, Morris Stoloff, Strongheart, Antole Litvak, Mark Serrurier Moviola, Pola Negri, Amelita Galli-Curci, John Bunny, and Yma Sumac.

Among the stars you will recognize, you'll wonder about their placement in the sidewalk. For instance, Marilyn Monroe's star is in front of a hole-in-the-wall fast-food joint, Bob Hope's marker is in the driveway of a car repair shop, while Gary Cooper's star is in front of a perpetually darkened bar that advertises some sort of frolic.

Mann's (formerly, Graumann's) Chinese Theater has more than handprints and footprints set in concrete. Roy Rogers also left the mark of his six-shooter and Trigger's horseshoes, while Gene Autry left horseshoe prints only. Jimmy Durante left the outline of his famous schnozz while Joe E. Brown left embedded in concrete a print of his mouth. Harold Lloyd left a sketch of his owlish glasses while Sonja Henie plunged her skate blades into concrete; George Burns and Milton Berle left impressions of stogies; Danny Thomas drew a cross, Bing Crosby sketched musical scales, and Gloria Swanson drew a heart with an arrow through it. Donald Duck left only his name and huge, webbed footprints.

Ever long for a more hands-on vacation treat? More excitement? Ever think about blowing up a building or riding in a supersonic jet? Do you have a *lot* of money? If so, Dreams Come True is a Hollywood firm that arranges that special, once-in-a-lifetime adventure. For instance, before you actually reduce a large building to rubble with high explosives in something known as the "Big Bang Weekend," you'll practice a few smaller dynamite explosions. The weekend "experience" teaches how explosions bring down a building. You take part in placing the explosives and then, on Sunday morning, actually push the plunger that triggers the blast. The Big Bang Weekend will also quickly reduce your wallet. Cost: $7500, dynamite included. A ride in a supersonic jet goes for $11,499 while a flight in a biplane that does stunts is only $300.

Every Saturday afternoon, the Scandals of D.C. Tour, in Washington, D.C., visits many famous places not marked by a monument. One place in history on the tour is the Sixth Street Southwest townhouse once owned by Gary Hart where he was extending overnight hospitality to Donna Rice when the Miami Herald happened along. Created by a local actors' group known as Gross National Product, the twenty-dollar tour also takes you to places where a congressman shot and killed his wife's lover, and where Representative Wilbur Mills followed exotic dancer Fanne Foxe into the waters of the Tidal Basin, out of power, and into Alcoholics Anonymous. An actor portraying Judge Ginsberg, who was yanked away from Supreme Court consideration when it was revealed the judge had once smoked pot, points out the "highest" court in the nation. There's a quick stop at the Vista Hotel where former Mayor Barry's career went up in the smoke of crack cocaine. The tour stops briefly at the point on the Capitol steps where Rita and John Jenrette made love in the moonlight. Other tour guides are actors who mimic George Bush, Fawn Hall (introduced as one of the greatest secretaries in American history), and Oliver North. A Richard Nixon-like character points out the Watergate building complex and its place in history. According to the tour, George Washington had a crush on a married woman and bought the pillows from her bed when she left the United States. The guided tour is offered on the Scandal Bus or you can drive yourself while listening to cassette tape.

While you're in Washington, you can follow the escape route traveled by John Wilkes Booth after he shot Abraham Lincoln on April 14, 1865. The tour starts at Ford's Theater in downtown Washington and follows the sixty-five to seventy-five mile escape route that took the assassin twelve days to travel before being captured and killed. Offered five or six times from April to September by the Surratt Society in Clinton, Maryland, the tour takes us moderns only twelve hours to cover the route by bus.

If money is no obstacle, there are many fantasy suites in hotels to stir your imagination. According to *Hotels* magazine, the most expensive hotel room in the Americas is the Galactic Fantasy Suite at the Crystal Palace Resort in Nassau, the Bahamas. The six-room suite has Ursula the Robot, a $125,000 device, to wait on you and explain how all the electronic devices in the suite operate. Ursula has been pre-programmed before your arrival and knows your name, favorite drink, sport, and video, which she fetches with an efficient whirr and hum. The suite offers an eight-foot wall of art that changes when you tire of it, a lucite piano that produces images as well as music, a rotary sofa and bed, and pulsating electric plasma sculptures. At night, the living-room ceiling offers four thousand points of fiber-optic starlight and a ringed Saturn. The windows are twenty feet tall and the place has a sixty-thousand-dollar audio-visual system for your listening and viewing pleasure. The master bedroom has an electronic thunder-and-lightning-storm device you can summon or stifle at will. The suite cost $1.36 million to build and costs the traveler twenty-five thousand dollars a night. According to the management, if you're an "aggressive gambler," (somebody who plays in the "mid–six-figure" range), the suite is all yours, courtesy of the house.

However, if your vacation budget happens to be less than the gross national product of most nations, there are other, more affordable fantasy suites. Various hotels offer: a Pharaoh's Chamber with painted hieroglyphics; an O.K. Corral hideaway, entered through a swinging gate; a Nature's Kingdom suite where you enter a tent to reach your bed; a thatched-roof Tahiti room; and a penthouse that looks like a prehistoric cave, complete with cave art, stalactites, and fur skins on the bed. In the Moby Dick Suite at the Burnsville Royale Hotel in Burnsville, Minnesota, you're greeted by the wide-open mouth of a whale. The same hotel offers rooms designed like a treehouse, a whaling ship, a sheik's tent, and a 1973 Olds. Still other hotels offer rooms based on the Tijuana jail; Tranquillity Base on the Moon; a huge igloo; a Hollywood nightclub; Sherwood Forest; a king-sized mock-up of a Gemini space capsule; a pickup truck; and a Cinderella suite that has your bed inside a horse-drawn carriage. The horse stays outside.

Many colleges and universities offer chances to work on far-flung, exotic research expeditions. They usually charge a fee, but the money can be counted as a tax-deductible contribution. For instance, William Franklin, an animal ecology professor, takes college students, outdoorsmen, senior citizens, and others to the wilds of Patagonia in Chile—where the Andean mountains meet the southern oceans and the Strait of Magellan—to study baby guanacos, an animal related to the llama. Most of the work consists of capturing and attaching eartags to newborn guanacos, then releasing them unharmed. Some volunteers work as "spotters," who are posted in the hills to watch for female guanacos giving birth. Side trips, strictly for pleasure, are made to penguin colonies and glacier-lined fjords and to the famous Inca ruins of Machu Picchu.

The University of California has a University Research Experience Program that sends vacationing volunteers to twenty to twenty-five scientific projects in as many nations. For instance, one study needs volunteers to help academics with a botanical collection in a rain forest in Ecuador; another needs assistants for an early-man dig in the People's Republic of China. For information, write: UREP, University of California, Desk NR, Berkeley, CA 94720. Or, call 415-642-6586.

A more accessible work vacation is the Tahoe Rim Trail Fund in Lake Tahoe, California, which takes volunteers to build and maintain a 150-mile hiking and riding trail at nine thousand feet around the lake, the largest and highest alpine lake in North America.

The Journey into American Indian Territory, headquartered in Westhampton Beach, New York, sets applicants up with one of sixty-six Indian nations in Oklahoma. For one week, vacationers live like nineteenth-century Plains Indians in teepees that must be set up, dismantled, moved, and assembled again. Nobody is required to bag a buffalo with a bow and arrow, but tour members do take part in ancient traditions like intertribal powwows, stomp dances, and other rituals not normally accessible to outsiders. Tour organizers also promise a lot of time for storytelling and hearing ancient Indian legends.

An appropriate trip on Halloween might be the Witches Trial Trail, a one-hour walking tour through Salem, Massachusetts, that shows what happened to some of the citizens charged with witchcraft in 1692. Among other displays and events, you can see re-creations of the twenty-two hangings and the one unfortunate who was pressed to death for practicing witchcraft. The organizers say it's a popular myth that convicted witches were burned. Original witch trials are reenacted with modern legal scholars making arguments on behalf of the accused.

Every year there are a handful of Thanksgiving attractions. At the Jamestown Settlement at Williamsburg, Virginia, some of the original American foods consumed by the Powhatan Indians

and the first English settlers are served at the attraction called
Foods and Feasts in Seventeenth Century Virginia. In the Mountain Man Rendezvous in Felton, California, Indians, fur trappers,
and traders of the American West show how things were done
around 1830 by performing Native American dances and throwing axes in contests. In Live Oak, Florida, at Spirit of the Suwan-
nee, there is the Old Tyme Farmers' Days celebration. You can
have Thanksgiving dinner and see how farmers of yesteryear made
sweet syrup from sugar cane and how they enjoyed games like
plough race where teams of mules, ploughs, and farmers raced.

After decades of domination by the New Year's celebration
in Times Square in New York City, the Space Needle in Seattle,
Washington, decided to become "Times Square of the West."

"West Coast residents need and want their own extravaganza
in their own time zone," says Kim Kimmy, spokeswoman.
"Watching New York's show on TV defeats the purpose. For us
in the West, the new year happens three hours later. Besides,
we never did like that ball that drops in Times Square."

Marked by three separate parties—smoke- and alcohol-free,
of course—the new year is observed when the specially lit north
elevator rises on the darkened Needle. It creates a streak of light
as thousands gather at the base of the Needle to count down to
zero. At precisely midnight, the elevator reaches the top of the
Space Needle and additional thousands of lights illuminate the
sky while a live band plays Auld Lang Syne.

In Mobile, Alabama, the great-granddaddy of all New Year
celebrations is held in the Cowbellion Herd New Year's Eve
Escapade and Revel. The celebration started in the first moments
of 1830 when a group of seven celebrating young men, led by
Michael Krafft, a handsome but one-eyed cotton broker, broke
into a hardware store to take cowbells and anything else that
would make noise. The celebrants got their name when a couple
of wags tied cowbells to the prongs of garden rakes. A passer-by
asked what was going on and Krafft quipped: "This is the Cow-

bellion de Rakin Society." The accepted New Year's custom of the time was to visit friends during the early evening hours of December 31 for a genteel cup of tea or punch. But The Cowbellions' middle-of-the-night ramblings ended on the doorstep of the mayor, into whose home they were reluctantly, and sleepily, invited for what historians have recorded only as "refreshments." The celebration continued in succeeding years and became known as an "Escapade." In 1834, lighted, decorated carts and buggies carrying masked revellers were added to the Escapade. By 1840, the group added an official theme, "Heathen Gods and Goddesses," to their parade. Later Cowbellion parades had themes like "The Darwinian Theory," and "Eras of the Crusades."

Because of the Civil War and Reconstruction, the parades became fewer and fewer and disappeared altogether around 1890. The Escapade in Mobile was recreated in 1987, again with theme parades. One year, the theme was "Herded Through the Grapevine," and had as its official seal an angry cow chasing a frightened raisin from a vineyard. Another year, the theme was "Cowabunga, Dude!" and featured a teenage mutant Ninja cow.

Now sponsored by the Resurrected Cowbellion de Rakin Society, the parade route and time are never announced except to Mobile's mayor, whose doorstep is again the final destination. And, yes, hizzoner has to invite everybody in for drinks. While serving a year's term, the president of the society is known as Michael Krafft III. (The original Krafft died of yellow fever in Pascagoula, Mississippi, in 1839, and never had children.)

The society says New Year's Eve and various Mardi Gras celebrations became noisy and boisterous after 1830 because the custom was imported to nearby New Orleans by several of Mobile's most dedicated Cowbellion members.

Krafft's body was eventually brought back to Mobile for reburial. His tall tombstone in Mobile's Magnolia Cemetery is something any tourist would like to see. It bears all the symbols of the original Cowbellions—the rake, a chamber pot, bell, and cow—all sculpted in marble.

11

THE WONDERFUL WORLD OF LITIGATION

William Howard Taft, president of the United States from 1909 to 1913 and, later, chief justice of the Supreme Court, was a huge man who weighted 330 pounds. One day, U.S. Senator Chauncey Depew was teasing Taft about the size of his stomach and asked if he was expecting a boy or a girl.

"Well, if it's a boy, I'll call him John," said Taft. "And if it's a girl, I'll call her Mary. But if, as I suspect, it's only wind, I'll call it Chauncey Depew."

Perhaps one of the chief sources of hot air in America can be found in our nation's courtrooms when lawsuits are argued. More and more Americans are using courtrooms, lawyers, and judges as their first, rather than last, resort when they are angry or even disgruntled.

For instance, the Nebraska Supreme Court ruled that watering a lawn does not take away your right to free speech.

When, in 1987, an anti-abortion activist in Omaha, Nebraska, picketed daily a building where two gynecologists practiced, the protester took it personally when the lawn sprinklers came on each morning and dampened the sidewalks. The protester filed suit, claiming the clinic was interfering with his right to free speech. The sprinklers, he claimed, forced him into the street to stay dry and made it more difficult to speak to women as they entered the clinic. The case made its way through the legal system to the Nebraska Supreme Court, required about four years to resolve, and cost the physicians about ten thousand dollars to defend.

"The taxpayers of Nebraska were also nicked about ten thousand dollars in costs for court time," says Larry Batt, the attorney who represented the clinic. "The protester who filed the action told the courts he wanted only to 'speak' to women entering the clinic, but he was there to harass patients going in for an abortion."

Yet another anti-abortion activist at the same clinic was halted in a hallway by a private security guard. Instead of fighting or resisting arrest, the sixty-seven-year-old protester feigned a heart attack. Doctors quickly learned the protester had not suffered a heart attack, but that he was soon due for one. The physicians found the protester had advanced heart disease, and a real heart attack was only a matter of time. Undaunted, the protester sued the clinic guard who arrested him.

A matter in Washington, D.C., has become known as "the cow pie case." The Foundation on Economic Trends is a Washington, D.C., action group that addresses issues concerning biotechnology. Among other matters, the foundation became concerned that flatulent livestock may be adding to global warming. When a cow (or sheep or buffalo) suffers an episode of digestive distress, the foundation notes, it passes methane gas into the atmosphere. Methane has been identified as contributing to global warming. The foundation alleged that flatulent livestock could be producing up to 15 percent of the methane in the upper skies, so it filed a lawsuit. The charge? The federal departments of Agriculture, Interior, and Energy have failed to measure how much damage livestock are doing to the atmosphere, and the suit asks the courts to order scientific studies to find exactly how much methane gas livestock are releasing. The foundation is also concerned with the gas content of the beasts' belches. If testing confirms a significant and damaging amount of methane is being released, the next step would be to encourage farmers to change their animals' feed, thereby making their belches and flatulence less gassy.

When Tom Gerner, D.D.S., was searching for a name for his five-man dental group in Plattsburg, New York, in 1981, he never thought it would become an issue before the courts.

"I was looking for a name that you would not forget immediately," Dr. Gerner says. "One of my friends hit on 'McDental.' I tried it out on people and found they remembered it two or three weeks later."

Things went along well until 1987, when the McDonald's corporation wrote a letter asking the dentists to drop the McDental name. In 1990, McDonald's filed suit.

McDental posted the charges for filling teeth, making bridges, doing extractions, and other procedures in their waiting room. McDonald's thought that it looked too much like one of their menus, so it mentioned that in their complaint as well.

"I don't think that McDonald's can claim to own every name that begins with 'Mc,' " Dr. Gerner says. "In my opinion, the firm is entirely humorless."

The matter of McDonald's v. McDental is continuing, thus far unresolved in the courts.

In 1985, a woman in Philadelphia walked into a mall and started shooting a rifle randomly. She struck ten people, killing three. The woman was found criminally insane and not responsible for her actions. A jury later ruled the crime was the fault of the mall, and that the shopping center was liable to the victims for damages. The exact amount of the award was kept secret.

During the trial, it was revealed that the woman—who had been in mental hospitals twelve times—had visited the mall before and had pointed her fingers like a gun and said "rat-tat-tat-tat." The woman made several more trips to the mall after that.

Counsel for the plaintiffs argued that there should have been more than one security guard on duty at the mall and that the shopping center should have foreseen the woman's actions because of her earlier odd behavior. But Lawrence Sherman, a criminologist at the University of Maryland and president of the Crime Control Institute in Washington, D.C., testified that from 1976 to 1984 crimes like the mall shooting occurred only about once a year in the United States. An average of seven people per year die from such crimes. Based on research of current crimes, Professor Sherman figured the odds of the plaintiffs dying in a mass murder were about one in 30 million. Moreover, the odds of the disturbed woman actually making good her threats were one in 156 million because such people rarely follow through. These odds were so low that Professor Sherman felt no reasonable person could have foreseen the shooting. Moreover, he felt the crime was impossible to prevent by any reasonable standards— the only way to have prevented a shooting attack at the mall would have been to turn it into an armed camp.

But the jury disagreed, and found for the plaintiffs.

The nation's first "wrongful life" suit was filed in 1990 when an eighty-two-year-old Cincinnati man was revived after a heart attack. The man had told his children and doctor that when his time came, they should simply let him die. But a medical team at St. Francis-St. George Hospital revived him with electric shock. Two days later, he suffered a debilitating stroke. The patient's lawyers sued for failing to follow his instructions, and for battery for giving him the jolt of electricity without his authorization. The court ruled there was no basis for a lawsuit based on keeping somebody alive.

Not all suits are matters of life and death. One action was brought because of a fear that people might confuse a movie with a gay street patrol. The Pink Panther Patrol in New York City was a street safety patrol operating in areas where gays have been bashed. When MGM-Pathe Communications, the company that owns the copyright to the *Pink Panther* movies and cartoons, found out about the patrol, they sued for copyright infringement. Result? The patrols are still out, helping to prevent gay bashing, but, after a judge's ruling, the gay group had to change its name. They are now known simply as "The Panthers."

The town of White River, Ontario, Canada, wanted to erect a statue of Winnie the Pooh because the character was based on a real bear born in White River. A Canadian soldier and veterinarian bought a black bear cub, tamed it, and took it to England during World War I as a brigade mascot. The bear was left at the London Zoo and became immensely popular when parents found the creature was so tame children could ride on its back. British writer A. A. Milne and his son, Christopher Robin, spent time with the bear in London. Milne later based his stories about Winnie the Pooh on the Canadian bear. The residents of White River discovered Pooh's origins and, in 1989, set out to build a twenty-five-foot statue of the bear. But the Disney corporation heard about it and stopped the project because they hold Pooh's copyright. However, the town has been persistent on the issue for several years and Disney may allow the statue to be built after all.

In yet another copyright infringement case, an entrepreneur in Texas came up with a new brand of prophylactics for men that he named "Stealth Condoms." Northrop Corporation, builder of the B-2 "stealth" bomber, filed suit, claiming people might confuse the two products.

Our environment is filled with potentially dangerous products or situations, and many suits are filed because someone was injured. For instance, an action for six million dollars was filed against the city of St. Joseph, Michigan, by a man who put his wife on the handlebars of his bicycle and took her for a ride. Unfortunately, the bike hit a pothole; the woman was pitched off and killed when she landed on her head. Her husband filed suit against the city because of the pothole, and the bicycle maker because the bike bore no warning label about giving somebody a ride on the handlebars. One bicycle manufacturer estimates there is one lawsuit for every two thousand bikes produced.

In Salt Lake City, a federal judge dismissed a lawsuit filed against the United States government by five vacationers who erected their tents on government property. The not-so-happy campers sued because they were injured when a hand grenade exploded in their campfire. The vacationers found a live hand grenade in the southern Utah desert and wondered what its explosion would be like. They took cover behind their cars as one threw the grenade into their campfire. Only the primer detonated—with a small pop—so everybody came out into the open. When the campers walked up to the campfire, the grenade exploded a second time and sprayed everybody with fragments, injuring them all.

Because of expensive lawsuits, many manufacturers are now cautioning their customers not to misuse their products, even in ways that require an incredible exercise of imagination. For instance, Proposition 65, a law in California, requires the public to be notified before anyone is exposed to a substance that has been shown to cause cancer or birth defects in laboratory mice or rats. A seemingly thoughtful law, but not thoughtful enough to stop the Los Angeles district attorney from suing three manufacturers of camping lanterns because their products did not carry warning labels. It seems there is a substance on the wick, which, if consumed in high enough quantities, could prove harmful, especially to rats and mice. When the courts settle the matter and the fines are dispensed, the lanterns will carry labels warning you not to chew on or eat the wicks.

One firm that makes and services towel machines for rest rooms carries on its machines the following: "Warning: Do not attempt to hang from towel, or insert your head into the towel loop. Failure to follow these simple instructions can be harmful or injurious." A cigarette lighter carried the following warning:

"Caution! Extinguish flame before reinserting in pocket or purse." Other lighters remind you not to leave the flame lit for over thirty seconds.

But there are always some who can find a way to do harm to themselves. For instance, two teenage girls in Maryland tried to make a scented candle by pouring perfume on a burning candle. The perfume burst into flames and burned one of the girls on the throat and breast. The girl's parents sued the perfume maker and won, when the judge ruled the company should have placed a warning on the perfume bottle. In another case, an extremely obese man went into a hospital for a stomach-stapling operation that would halve the size of his stomach and help him lose weight because it would not be able to hold as much food. One night after the operation, the patient sneaked into the hospital kitchen, gobbled down a hearty snack, and later popped the staples holding his incision. The patient sued the hospital for one-quarter million dollars, claiming the medics should never have allowed him access to their refrigerator. The patient lost the case.

"Behind many product liability suits is an assumption that we should live in a completely risk-free society, that people should be able to do anything with any product, and that's not logical," says Anne Allen of the American Tort Reform Association in Washington, D.C.

Of course, there are always at least a few people who really do need to be protected from themselves. For instance, a man in Florida fought for almost two years to keep two alligators in his home as pets. Officers from Florida's Department of Fish and Game visited the man's home to check on his living quarters after he filed for a permit to keep the creatures in November, 1989. It turned out to be a bad time for a visit. The officers found both alligators in the applicant's bed. Moreover, the 'gator lover was bleeding from bites on his legs. The officers promptly denied the man's application to keep the alligators, confiscated the creatures, and left the applicant with a citation. He then sued to get his property back, complaining his pets had been taken without a hearing. The man won two lower-court hearings but the state appealed each time. Finally, an appeals court ruled it is indeed illegal in Florida to keep alligators in one's bed. The applicant did not get his pets back.

Sometimes a well-meaning citizen does a good deed only to see it backfire. When a San Francisco cabdriver captured an armed mugger, he used his taxi to chase and pin the man against the wall of a building. The mugger had just beaten and robbed a Japanese tourist and was trying to run away, but the cabdriver held him for police. In court, the robber pleaded guilty to robbery and was sentenced to eight years in the state prison. That didn't stop him from suing the cabdriver and the driver's employer, Luxor Cab Company, for using excessive force and breaking his leg in the capture. The mugger is asking a court for five million dollars in damages. Just after the capture, the driver, who has driven cabs for twenty-four years and also works as a stunt driver for television and the movies, said he used his cab to pin and hold the robber because he thought he saw a gun in the man's hand. "The case is making it much more expensive for us to do business," says Mary Warner, vice-president of Luxor.

A jury ordered the cabdriver to pay twenty-five thousand dollars for injuries to the robbers' legs.

After Madeline D. Sitzes, a lawyer in Houston, Texas, spent half an hour giving artificial respiration to a woman who had quit breathing and passed out in the hallway of a courthouse, three fire department paramedics refused to take the woman to the hospital because of severe budget cutbacks. The rescue was difficult because the woman had no pulse and her jaws were locked shut, so Sitzes had to blow air through her nose. But the paramedics would not put the woman in the ambulance.

"I kept arguing and trying to convince them this woman was desperately ill," says Ms. Sitzes. "One of the paramedics stood on my toes to shut me up, and when I told him to get the hell off, he ground his foot down into mine even harder. So I kicked him in the shin with my other foot."

After having saved a stranger's life, Sitzes then found herself charged with criminal assault for having kicked the paramedic. The district attorney pleaded with him, but he would not drop the case. Sitzes was tried before a judge who found her not guilty after a five-hour trial. About a dozen Houston-area attorneys offered to represent Sitzes without charge.

"At the time, I think the paramedics were under pressure not to take poor people to the hospital because our medical facilities for the indigent here were somewhat overwhelmed," Sitzes says.

When the Riverside Mountain Rescue Unit went to the aid of a mountain climber, they found the man had fallen ninety feet onto boulders and had hung upside down for over twenty-four hours. The volunteer rescue unit includes physicians and paramedics and has saved hundreds of lives over thirty years. They found the only way to avoid pulling the injured man up a steep, bumpy, eight-hundred-foot slope was to rescue him with a helicopter, so the tricky rescue was done at night in high winds. Two years later, the accident victim filed a twelve-million-dollar lawsuit, saying reckless and negligent rescue techniques had caused him the loss of the use of his legs. The suit named the rescue unit, the private pilot, the forest service, the county, the hospital, and anybody else that had anything at all to do with the rescue. The suit was eventually dropped, but everybody in the rescue unit lost many hours from work to attend legal proceedings. Moreover, the rescue unit is now required to fill out much more documentation and other paperwork in case other lawsuits are filed. This slows them down on rescues in the field.

"We tried to find liability insurance several years ago, but the only firm that would insure us was Lloyd's of London and they wanted $120,000 to insure our team," says Walter Walker, one of the organizers of the rescue unit. "Our operating budget for a year is only $25,000. The insurance companies tell us accident victims routinely sue when the rescue teams have done nothing at all to cause their injuries."

Sometimes, the subjects of lawsuits are more personal in nature. A case in Texas involves fake nipples used to circumvent a ruling by the U.S. Supreme Court.

To check the spread of topless bars, city fathers in Dallas drafted an ordinance that requires topless bars to be at least one thousand feet from churches, schools, neighborhoods, historic districts, and other sexually oriented businesses.

The U.S. Supreme Court upheld the right of state and local governments to ban nude dancing, but suggested that restrictions on pasties and G-strings would violate free speech. Topless-bar owners in Texas then started applying flesh-colored pasties to the breasts of their dancers. Customers couldn't tell the difference and neither could police. To see if the law was being violated, vice officers have dancers leave the stage and peel off the pasties.

Beliefs are often tested in the courtroom. Twin ten-year-old Cub Scouts in Orange, California, refused to say the word "God" in the Cub Scout Promise to ". . . do my duty to God . . ." because they are atheists. The boys were then booted out of the organization. The family sued the Boy Scouts of America, saying the organization had violated their children's freedom of religion. Counsel for the Boy Scouts maintains that the Scouts is a private group whose members should not be required to associate with those who do not accept the organization's moral tenets. A judge ordered that the boys be temporarily reinstated in the organization while he takes a final decision under advisement.

Sometimes, matters of taste are brought into the courtroom. When Lynn Rasmussen decided to name her restaurant "Okie Girl," the California Department of Transportation felt the name might offend travelers from Oklahoma or the many stalwart citizens of California who had fled the Dust Bowl in the 1930s and made the Golden State their new home. Consequently, the state would not erect signs about the "Okie Girl" restaurant on the freeway as they routinely do for other such roadside businesses. Because Rasmussen is from Oklahoma, she felt the name of the restaurant was completely appropriate and sued the Department of Transportation. A superior court later ordered signs about the restaurant to be posted on the freeway. Moreover, Rasmussen received $32,500 to compensate for freeway travelers who had bypassed her restaurant.

In 1983, an Eastern Airlines plane lost power and the pilot told the passengers to prepare for a crash landing. But the engines restarted and the plane landed safely. Some passengers sued nonetheless, saying they had been traumatized by fear. A federal court ruled the passengers could win damages if they could prove they had suffered emotional injuries because of the fear caused by the near-crash. But the U.S. Supreme Court reversed that finding in a 9-0 decision, saying white knuckles aren't enough to collect damages. You must suffer an actual injury to the body.

The city of San Diego was once sued for NOT arresting a motorcycle rider. A police officer stopped a motorcycle for speeding and gave the rider a ticket. Shortly thereafter, the rider crashed his bike and was seriously injured. While testing his blood, doctors found the man was legally drunk. The police officer testified he had no indication that the rider had been drinking. The rider's lawyer argued that the injured rider was lulled into a false sense of security because he was not arrested. A court of appeals found the city not liable.

Some lawsuits seemingly grasp at straws. Back in 1777, while fighting the Revolutionary War, George Washington and his army fell on hard times at Valley Forge. The Continental Congress asked citizens for loans and promised to repay the money, plus interest. A wealthy Philadelphia merchant, Jacob

DeHaven, responded and lent the fledgling government almost everything he owned. His gold and various supplies amounted to about 450,000 Revolutionary dollars. DeHaven died childless and in poverty in 1812. In 1987, descendants of DeHaven's brother asked the United States government for the return of the $450,000—plus 212 years of compounded interest, an amount which would come to about $98.3 billion, if the interest were compounded annually. If the interest were compounded daily, the heirs wanted $141.6 billion. The lawyer argued for the claimants: "What Jacob DeHaven loaned the government was then the equivalent of the Pentagon budget. He virtually underwrote the war at Valley Force." The matter was never heard in DeHaven's time because early America copied English law, in which governments could not be sued. In 1859, a special court was created to hear claims against the government. In 1991, the U.S. Court of Appeals ruled the statute of limitations for loans made to the father of the nation had expired in 1865.

When a California woman lost her dog, she offered a reward of twenty-five hundred dollars. Weeks later, a couple showed up at the woman's door with the bones of a dog they found in the neighborhood. The former pet owner refused to pay, so the finders of the bones sued. A judge found for the pet owner.

A superior court case involved a woman and a carpet layer. After contractors had installed her carpet, the woman noticed her piggy bank was missing. She complained to the crew's supervisor and he found one of his men had indeed filched the piggy bank, which contained five or six dollars. The thief was fired on the spot. The homeowner filed papers anyhow, suing for loss of property for the two hours the carpet layer had possession of her piggy bank. She lost the case.

Many times, lawsuits are filed because somebody's feelings have been hurt—and their ruffled feathers just can't be easily smoothed.

When The Judds, a mother-daughter duo who have won some of country music's top awards, gave their final concert, it was an emotional and often weepy affair because Naomi Judd, the mother, was being forced into retirement because of chronic hepatitis, a liver disease that can be fatal. Completely unmoved, a former Judd fan filed suit saying he and others had paid twenty-five dollars for a three-hour, pay-per-view show but had only received two hours. The complaining fan said his attorney will seek reimbursement in a class-action suit and may ask for punitive damages. Named in the suit are forty-five-year-old Naomi Judd and her daughter Wynonna, twenty-seven, the firm that distributed the program, the program's promoter, and others. The proceedings will probably drag on for years.

A dispute over $9.89 once tied up a Lone Star court for three weeks. A seventy-eight-year-old grandmother from McKinney, Texas, bought a used pickup truck from a dealership, but the dealer made a mistake in the paperwork and figured the financing at an interest rate of 26.75 percent instead of 26.58 percent. The error cost the woman $9.89 more. The grandmother sued, saying the dealership charged her an illegally high interest rate. The suit asked for $30,000 in damages from the dealership and its president. But the dealership said the grandmother had used false information on her request for credit and countersued, seeking $50,000 for damages. It took eleven days for the trial, two days for attorneys' conferences and a day for arguments. The four-woman, two-man jury decided the mistake had been made in good faith and that neither side would receive the awards they had asked for. The grandmother was awarded the $9.89 while the two attorneys who represented her at different times waived their fees. But the dealership is no longer in business.

When the United States and its allies went to war in the Persian Gulf, a couple hung an American flag to show their support for the troops. Their landlord, a Jehovah's Witness, felt the flag represented a false idol and evicted them. The couple then filed suit. The case is still pending.

A traveling stand-up comedian moved in with his girlfriend. Each owned two cats. The comedian traveled often so the girlfriend cared for the four felines. After two and a half years, the romance ended and the girlfriend took off with all four cats. The comedian asked for the return of his pets but she refused, saying the five had become "family." He sued, asking for twenty-four thousand dollars, which was one hundred dollars a day per cat, for loss of companionship. Depositions were filed with each party's lawyer but the girlfriend finally relented and returned her boyfriend's two cats, saying the stress and expense had become too much.

When a twenty-eight-year-old college student in Orlando, Florida, got a twelve-dollar haircut at a J. C. Penney salon, he later filed a lawsuit asking for ten thousand dollars in damages. He complained that the company stylist had botched the job so badly that he was deprived of his right to enjoy life, ridiculed by his friends, and forced to wear a hat, give up dating, and seek psychiatric counseling. He charged the haircut was so bad and he was so traumatized that he didn't leave his home for three days. Attorneys for J. C. Penney made a motion to dismiss the suit and the judge quickly granted it.

In Michigan, a seventeen-year-old girl claimed she suffered an inflamed thumb from playing too much Nintendo. Her family sued Nintendo and the Toys "Я" Us outlet where she had bought the game. The girl complained to the court of an inflamed thumb, a condition a physician and expert witness later named "Nintendinitis." The girl complained that the injured thumb interfered with her schoolwork because she could not hold a pencil or type. The matter is pending.

In Pennsylvania, a man who was arrested on drug charges later sued the police department because, at the time of the arrest, he was making love with his wife. The suit charged that the police violated his right to privacy by interrupting him in bed and arresting him. A Pennsylvania appeals court decided the police did not have to guarantee a suspect safe sex and that the police acted properly.

In California, a sleepy lawyer asked his next door neighbor, also a lawyer, to quit playing basketball in his driveway so he could take a nap. But the game went on. So the nap-deprived lawyer sprayed the basketball-playing lawyer with a hose. The dampened party then sued, claiming emotional distress. The neighbor countersued, complaining the basketball-loving lawyer had reduced the value of his home. Eventually, a court issued a permanent injunction, limiting play to six hours of basketball daily. A state appeals court then lifted the injunction saying the noise could be reduced by closing the window. The matter is still unresolved and headed for another court.

In Tennessee, the skin of a newborn was accidentally and temporarily dyed blue when a blue dye was injected into the mother to test for a urinary tract infection twelve hours before she went into labor. When the healthy baby girl was born, workers at the hospital nicknamed her a "Smurfette." The couples' lawyer then filed a suit for four million dollars, saying the mother was subjected to the callous, distressing remarks about having a "Smurfette." That, in turn, caused "extreme, distressing, and permanent emotional damage, humiliation, and ridicule." The case is pending.

In a championship tennis match featuring John McEnroe, a spectator in the stands jeered at the often ill-tempered player. McEnroe walked to where the fan was sitting and threw his predictable shouting fit. The fan then filed a suit, claiming six million dollars in damages. The judge tossed the matter out after hearing opening (but calm) arguments.

Most sex-discrimination suits have been filed by women, but there's always the occasional surprise. For instance, a Bronx house-husband took care of the baby while his wife worked. The man spotted an ad inviting new mothers to bring their babies and get together to chat. The house-husband called and asked about joining, but was told the group was taking no new members. The next day, his wife called and was invited to attend the group. The husband filed a sexual-discrimination complaint because the mothers' group is publicly funded. The case is under consideration.

Andrew Exler, a civil-rights activist and a paralegal from Palm Springs, California, went to Disneyland in California in 1980 with his date, another man. Park officials told the pair there was a ban on same-sex dancing and then asked them to leave the park. Exler sued. In 1984, a judge found Exler and his date had been discriminated against. The following year, Disney announced they would permit same-sex "touch" dancing after all. In fact, when Exler returned to dance at the Magic Kingdom nine years later, a security guard asked if he was having any problems at all with the guests.

In 1988, Exler and two friends went to a Chippendales nightclub to see male exotic dancers, but were denied entrance because the show was for women only. Exler sued again. The nightclub later settled with Exler, gave him an undisclosed amount of money, a letter of apology, and a promise that men would be admitted to the show.

In 1990, Exler, who was by now seriously thinking of becoming an attorney, went to a Hollywood dance club on miniskirt night. Patrons who wore a mini did not have to pay a $10 cover charge. But Exler, another man, and a woman—all wearing slacks—were denied the free entrance and later filed suit, seeking $1 million in punitive damages and $250 in actual damages for humiliation and degradation. A court later ruled that breaks in price based on sex-based dress regulations are illegal.

When a restaurant in Palm Springs started advertising price breaks on meals for senior citizens, Exler sued because of age discrimination, but a judge ruled against him. Exler appealed the case. Then, when Exler decided he would like to lose some weight, he went to a Gloria Marshall Figure Salon. The salon told him the chain only serves women. Once again, Exler sued, this time for $1 million in damages.

"I don't see any difference between what I'm doing and what Rosa Parks did when she refused to get up and go to the back of the bus," Exler says. "My lawsuits are about civil rights, not money. For instance, if Gloria Marshall would change its discriminatory policy against men, I would drop the suit."

In 1984, a lesbian couple went to Papa Chouc, a posh French restaurant in Los Angeles. The eatery had eight curtained booths for extra-romantic dining but refused to seat the couple in one. A discrimination suit was filed and a judge ruled against the couple. But a higher court agreed the couple had been subjected to illegal discrimination and ordered the restaurant to admit all amorous couples to curtained booths.

Sometimes just the fear of a lawsuit can bring a sizable reward. When two female bodybuilders went to a Billy Idol concert in Costa Mesa, California, they were stopped near a women's rest room by two policemen who had been called to investigate a call about men using the ladies' room. Because the women had developed such large muscles by lifting weights, the policemen didn't believe they were really females. The cops called over a female security guard and told the pair to drop their drawers and prove their gender. One woman had her driver's license to prove her sex but her friend had left her ID in the car. The twenty-eight-year-old woman lowered her pants and proved beyond any reasonable doubt that she was indeed a female. The next day, an attorney for the two body builders filed suit, asking damages for emotional distress, violation of civil rights, defamation, assault and battery, and false imprisonment. The suit sought $1 million. After a year of legal wrangling, the city paid the first woman $20,000 and $45,000 to the woman who lowered her pants.

*   *   *

Jeffrey B. Nugent, a professor of economics at the University of Southern California, once compared the economies and numbers of lawyers in fifty-two nations. His findings? The higher the percentage of lawyers in a nation's labor force, the lower that country's economic growth rate. The study, printed in the professional journal *World Development*, suggests that nations might have faster economic growth if they reduced the percentage of lawyers and encouraged more young people to enter more productive fields.

For instance, Japan, South Korea, and Taiwan all have low numbers of lawyers, and their economies are among the world's fastest growing. Nations like the United States, England, Canada, and Israel have low rates of economic growth and high percentages of lawyers.

"Much of what lawyers do is sue people," Dr. Nugent says. "One result is that, in the United States, our auto insurance rates are very high. When lawyers sue manufacturers, the price of their products must go up to cover high legal costs. Also, many legislators are lawyers, and they write legislation that requires lawyers to interpret."

But the United States is not the only nation in which picayune lawsuits are heard.

When welfare officials would not increase his twenty-deutsche marks (DM) monthly allotment for condoms, a twenty-nine-year-old welfare recipient in Hamburg, Germany, sued to have his benefits increased so he could purchase what he considered a necessary number of prophylactics. (DM20 is about $12.42.)

"My girlfriend and I have sex an average of 1.7 times a day," stated the complainant, who added that DM20 only buys twenty condoms. He sued for an increase in the condom allotment to DM47.80 (about $30.00), arguing that the courts and welfare system could not "dictate how often I sleep with my girlfriend."

The court ruled against the recipient, writing that the welfare system is not required to provide recipients with "complete fulfillment of all their needs." With proper Teutonic thoroughness, the justices also showed how the recipient could—no pun intended—stretch his condom budget.

If he saved his monthly allowance for three months, the judges reckoned, he could buy a bulk package of a hundred and fifty at a discount store, giving him fifty per month, about what he had figured was needed in the first place.